Engaging Diverse College Alumni

Changing demographics are having a substantial impact on college and university student populations. In order to continue garnering funds and supporting their higher education institutions, development offices and individual fundraisers need to learn more about alumni of color. To help move fundraising staff away from a "one size fits all" approach, *Engaging Diverse College Alumni* provides a comprehensive overview of philanthropy in diverse cultures. Unlike other works on fundraising within communities of color, this book focuses specifically on college and university alumni and offers concrete suggestions for engaging these populations, including best practices as well as approaches to avoid.

This practical guide includes:

- A Comprehensive Overview of Diverse Cultures – use of secondary sources, interviews, and quantitative data to explore the history, motivations, and trends of Latino, African American, Native American, and Asian American and Pacific Islander communities.
- Practical Recommendations – data-based recommendations and examples integrated throughout the chapters, including "Strategies at a Glance" for quick reference.
- Best Practices and Innovative Approaches – interviews with advancement staff and alumni of color, an entire chapter outlining successful innovative fundraising programs, and a chapter on common pitfalls to avoid.

Both newcomers and seasoned fundraising professionals will find this book to be a compelling and in-depth guide to engaging diverse college alumni.

Marybeth Gasman is Professor of Higher Education in the Graduate School of Education at the University of Pennsylvania, USA.

Nelson Bowman III is Executive Director of Development at Prairie View A&M University, USA.

D1547712

ENGAGING DIVERSE COLLEGE ALUMNI

THE ESSENTIAL GUIDE TO FUNDRAISING

Marybeth Gasman and
Nelson Bowman III

Routledge
Taylor & Francis Group

NEW YORK AND LONDON

First published 2013
by Routledge
711 Third Avenue, New York, NY 10017

Simultaneously published in the UK
by Routledge
2 Park Square, Milton Park, Abingdon, Oxon OX14 4RN

Routledge is an imprint of the Taylor & Francis Group, an informa business

© 2013 Taylor & Francis

Library of Congress Cataloging-in-Publication Data
Gasman, Marybeth.
Engaging diverse college alumni : the essential guide to
fundraising / by Marybeth Gasman and Nelson Bowman III.
    pages cm
    Includes bibliographical references and index.
1. Educational fund raising–United States. 2. Education,
Higher–United States–Finance. 3. Universities and
colleges–Alumni and alumnae–United States. I. Title.
LB2336.G36 2013
371.2'06–dc23   2012037599

ISBN: 978–0–415–89274–2 (hbk)
ISBN: 978–0–415–89275–9 (pbk)
ISBN: 978–0–203–81760–5 (ebk)

Typeset in Minion
by Swales & Willis Ltd, Exeter, Devon

Printed and bound in the United States of America
by Edwards Brothers, Inc.

In loving memory of
Nelson (Nelse) Bowman, Jr.
1924–2011

CONTENTS

ACKNOWLEDGMENTS

We began working on this book several years ago. It was born out of a series of talks that we gave together at conferences as well as colleges and university campuses across the country. Both of us had been writing and presenting on African American philanthropy for quite some time and, due to the changing demographics of the nation and the many questions we received from people throughout the country, we decided to start thinking more about other racial and ethnic groups and their philanthropic endeavors. What we found is that even though there is a growing body of research on philanthropy in communities of color, there is almost no research and barely a conversation on engaging alumni of color, especially at majority institutions. The philanthropy and foundation world started a conversation around donors of color in the late 1990s and early 2000s, but the fundraising world never listened, including colleges and university development and alumni offices (Council on Foundations, 1999; W. K. Kellogg Foundation, 2001). American institutions of higher education are rapidly changing in terms of students and alumni and college and university development offices are not prepared. People are having an occasional conversation about the need to diversify their fundraising staffs or the changing student body at their institutions, but they are not taking any action based on these conversations. They are not changing their strategies and approaches to fundraising.

We both care about the experiences of all students in higher education and especially students of color. Likewise, we care about their experiences once they graduate and become alumni. We think that colleges and universities should care about their alumni of color as well and, as a result, we wrote this book to demonstrate the power of giving among people of color and alumni of color and to provide ideas, suggestions, and evidence that alumni of color can and will contribute to the future of colleges and universities.

We had much assistance in researching this book and are grateful to the following graduate students and research assistants for their help on this project: Thai-Huy Nguyen, Shana Yem, Nina Daoud, Danielle Forsythe, Felecia Commodore, Claire Fluker, and Stephen Garlington. Each of these students helped to gather data for our book. We appreciate their suggestions, input, and good spirits throughout this process. We are also grateful to Heather Jarrow, our editor at Routledge. She is wonderfully thorough and gives terrific feedback.

We are also thankful to all of the college and university development and alumni staff members that agreed to participate in interviews and completed our survey. Without them we would not have an understanding of how colleges and universities engage and solicit alumni of color. Through these individuals we were able to capture what is being done and what is being overlooked. Likewise, we are grateful to the hundreds of alumni of color that completed our online survey about their experiences and how they want to be engaged and solicited.

Lastly, we are appreciative of one another and to our families for the support during this writing process. Through our friendship, we try to demonstrate collaboration across many areas, including race, gender, and place in higher education.

Coming together with someone who has different interests and perspectives makes anything produced much stronger. We were fortunate that during the writing of this book, there was a lot of laughter and even more learning. We look forward to future collaborations.

1

INTRODUCTION

The U.S. traditional models and expectations of charitable giving were developed by white men, and these may not reflect philanthropy in other cultures because minorities do not give for the same reasons white men do.

Wagner & Ryan, 2004, p. 66

The face of philanthropy is rapidly changing to become as ethnically, culturally and socioeconomically diverse as our country's population, with some of the most significant growth stemming from identity-based philanthropy—a growing movement to spark philanthropic giving from a community on behalf of a community, where "community" is defined by race, ethnicity, gender or sexual orientation.

W. K. Kellogg Foundation, 2012

The United States is becoming more racially and ethnically diverse (U.S. Census, 2010). This increased diversity reflects two forces. First, immigration has been a major influence on both the size and the age structure of the population. Although most immigrants arrive as young adults, when they are most likely and willing to assume the risks of moving to a new country, U.S. immigration policy has also favored the entry of parents and other family members of these young immigrants. Second, major racial and ethnic groups are aging at different rates, depending upon fertility, mortality, and immigration within these groups. According to the 2010 Census, by 2050, our nation will be majority minority – with all of the people of color combined outnumbering the White population. One can see evidence of this change already, as there were more babies of color born in 2012 than White babies (U.S. Census, 2010). Latinos and Asians are growing at the fastest rate. Figures 1.1 and 1.2 depict the changing demographics in the country.

These changing demographics are already having a substantial impact on college and university student populations. Consider Table 1.1, which details the undergraduate population.

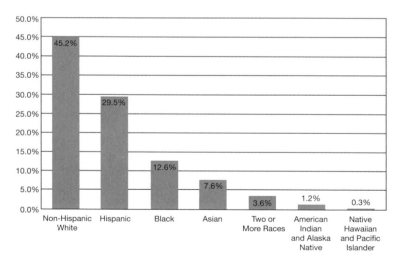

Figure 1.1 Population projections by race for 2050 (Census Bureau).

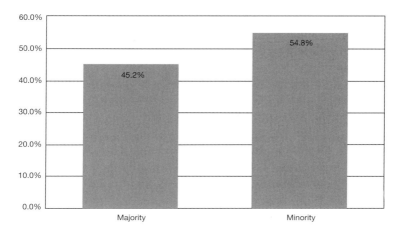

Figure 1.2 Population projections – majority/minority for 2050 (Census Bureau).

These data show overwhelming growth between 1984 and 2009 for Latinos, Asians, Blacks, and even Native Americans within higher education student enrollment.

METHODS BEHIND THE STUDY

Unfortunately, there is very little data related to philanthropic giving among alumni of color. Most institutions do not collect this data nor does the Council for the Support and Advancement of Education (CASE). As a result, the field knows almost nothing about the way alumni of color engage, give, and volunteer.

In order to secure data for this book, we used several approaches. First, we carried out a comprehensive review of the literature on philanthropy in communities of color, drawing from the fields of philanthropic studies, history, sociology, and ethnic studies. We drew from all of this literature to provide readers with a thorough overview of philanthropic trends in diverse communities. We also consulted literature on alumni

Table 1.1 National enrollment, race/ethnicity

National Enrollment, Race/Ethnicity	2009			1984		
	Change	UG	Total	UG	Total	
American Indian or Alaska Native	219%	245,843	267,100	–	83,694	
Asian/Native Hawaiian/Other Pacific Islander	314%	1,410,011	1,611,468	–	389,679	
Black or African American/Black non-Hispanic	240%	3,281,901	3,663,713	–	1,076,000	
Hispanic or Latino/Hispanic	546%	3,223,841	3,455,505	–	535,155	
White/White non-Hispanic	56%	13,215,215	15,284,867	–	9,815,012	
Race/Ethnicity Unknown	–	2,082,104	2,558,021	–	–	
Non-Resident Alien	146%	470,211	823,933	–	334,705	
Total	Total	23,929,126	27,664,607	–	12,234,245	

Source: IPEDS

giving and fundraising in general, drawing best practices from the mainstream literature. In order to understand how and why alumni of color give, it is vital to understand the cultural nuances of the various communities of color.

Next, we interviewed development and alumni staff at 19 institutions (see Appendix B) out of the 61 members of the American Association of Universities (see Appendix A). We chose the institutions to interview based on an examination of all of the member institutions' programs (or lack thereof) for alumni of color. We chose those institutions with at least one program for alumni of color and also sought institutions representing a cross-section of the nation. We interviewed several members of the development and alumni relations staffs at each institution. At institutions where the office of diversity worked hand in hand with institutional advancement, we also interviewed the chief diversity officer. We have identified these individuals by name in the book as we secured their permission to do so. The interview questions are included in Appendix C.

Of note, several institutions refused to participate in the interviews, expressing fear in terms of the public perception of their efforts, or more so lack of efforts. This fear demonstrates that institutions are still deeply uncomfortable talking about race and racial issues.

In addition to the interviews, we surveyed all of the AAU member institution Vice Presidents of Institutional Advancement using Survey Monkey. Thirty-four of the vice presidents answered the survey, giving us a 55.7 percent response rate. Each survey respondent completed all of the survey questions. The survey is included in Appendix D.

We also surveyed alumni of color about their experiences (see Appendix E). We distributed the survey using Survey Monkey to 800 alumni of color from institutions across the country and had a 35.8 percent response rate.

Lastly, we reviewed the websites of all of the AAU member institutions, looking for model programs for engaging and soliciting alumni of color. These programs are included in a separate chapter of the book.

IDENTIFYING THE PROBLEM

Higher education fundraisers are ill-equipped in their ability to cultivate these growing populations. They have long engaged and solicited mainly White alumni and know almost nothing about philanthropy and fundraising within diverse cultures. Moreover, most fundraising staffs lack fundraisers of color. According to the Association of Fundraising Professionals (AFP) and the Council for the Support and Advancement of Education (CASE), both recognized as leading professional associations for advancement professionals, only 11 and 10 percent, respectively, of their registered members are people of color. This information is further validated in the research conducted for this project. We surveyed the 61 member institutions of the Association of American Universities (AAU) about employee diversity within their fundraising shops and the results clearly speak to the need for more fundraisers of color. On average the AAU institutions surveyed had 17 percent people of color on their staffs, with one institution boasting a staff that is 25 percent people of color and another having only 6 percent people of color. The problem is that very few of these individuals are front-line fundraisers.

An example from our survey that stood out and corroborates the demographic shift on college campuses is a school that currently has a student population that is 62 percent students of color and an alumni base that is 54 percent alumni of color (since 1993) and yet their development staff is only 15 percent people of color, with two front line fundraisers of color. One may argue that having fundraisers of color is not an absolute requirement for cultivating people of color, and that is true. However, our research shows that people of diverse cultures and ethnic groups tend to embrace and, in many cases, prefer to be cultivated by individuals of the same race or ethnic make-up. Question: in business, when companies notice that the demographic they cater to is changing, they quickly adjust the marketing, packaging, and personnel to ensure no loss of, and the possibility of increased, sales. So why would an institution of higher education, sharing a similar need of wanting to increase funding, not follow that same business model?

According to Emmett D. Carson (as quoted in Kasper, Ramos, & Walker, 2004), the bottom line when it comes to diversity is the "two M's: morality and market" (p. 3). Reaching out to alumni of color is not only the right thing to do, it is a necessity as most colleges and universities are no longer predominantly White. Fundraisers do not want to alienate any of their alumni, as the goal is to garner funds to support their institutions. Those having doubts about diversifying within the area of fundraising, should consider that the world and the United States are rapidly changing in terms of demographics as noted earlier. Also consider that individuals give the majority of money to nonprofits and as these individuals are changing with regard to race and ethnicity, they will need to be engaged. Unfortunately, most colleges and universities are not prepared for this engagement (Gough, 2001; Hendricks, 1998; Klein, 1998).

Development offices and individual fundraisers need to modify their "one size fits all" approach to cultivating alumni in order to capture or in some cases recapture the affinity of their graduates of color. While this shift may seem obvious in a changing world, the fundraising establishment has been slow to formally recognize the need for change. Both philanthropy and fundraising researchers have been sluggish about creating research-based tools and providing scholarly understanding of philanthropy in diverse cultures. A quick scan of CASE's or AFP's conference programs will demonstrate that these organizations need to increase their commitment to philanthropy in communities of color. On average there are only one or two sessions, if that, dedicated to diversity in fundraising. And, as we have led many of these sessions, we know that the audiences are typically people of color rather than the traditional members of CASE and AFP that desperately need this education. When will mainstream fundraisers within these organizations begin to realize that it is important to engage alumni of color? Many times when we ask this question to audiences at national conferences, they say that they will begin to do it when they have data that show that alumni of color give. There is ample data that show that people of color give and give generously, but this data needs to be consulted (Duran, 2001; Nichols, 2008). Most fundraisers are White and the growing student (and thus alumni) body is becoming more and more diverse. This fact begs the question: how will these fundraisers be successful in terms of raising monies for their institutions? Will they understand the nuances involved in engaging and soliciting alumni of color? With little exposure to cultures other than the majority culture, college and university fundraisers will likely attempt a "cookie cutter approach" to fundraising and fail amongst alumni of color, especially those that are first generation, which will be the majority of them (National Center for Education Statistics, 2010).

To help move fundraising staffs away from a "one size fits all" approach, our book provides a comprehensive overview of philanthropy in diverse cultures, including African Americans, Asian Americans and Pacific Islanders, Latinos, and Native Americans. We delve deeply into the history, motivations, and trends of each racial and ethnic community using secondary sources, interviews, and quantitative data. Unlike other work on philanthropy within communities of color, our book focuses on college and university alumni and offers concrete suggestions for cultivating and soliciting these populations. We present many examples of best practices at various types of colleges and universities as well as practices to avoid.

CHECKING THE PULSE OF YOUR INSTITUTION

As you read this book, it will be beneficial to think about your own institution and how it fares in terms of the questions below. If you cannot answer these questions, you most likely need to make some changes to better prepare for the changing alumni population.

1. **What percentage of your alumni is represented by people of color?** Do you keep track of this information? How often do you collect information on your alumni in terms of race and ethnicity? How has your alumni changed over time?
2. **What are the current levels of giving from minority alumni?** How does their giving compare to giving overall?
3. **What staff positions support your work targeting alumni of color?** Are fundraisers of color on your staff? Are they the only ones who are reaching out to alumni of color? Do all fundraisers have a responsibility to reach out to alumni of color? Are they trained to be sensitive to the needs and cultural traditions of alumni of color?
4. **Which minority affinity groups do you currently target through your fundraising efforts?** Are all of your groups equally strong? Do you have alumni of color who are leaders of these groups? Are these individuals active in the general alumni events? Are they encouraged to be involved and active?
5. **What have you done so far to reach and engage alumni of color?** What efforts do you currently have in place? How successful are these events? Does the president or vice president of advancement attend these events? Do you have

special programs rooted in the experiences of various racial and ethnic groups on your campus?

6. **What student programs on campus are geared toward alumni of color?** Do these programs regularly invite alumni back to campus as speakers for graduation or special events? Does the advancement office connect with these programs to co-host activities? Do you tap the student leaders involved in these events to become alumni leaders?

7. **Does your institution's marketing include alumni of color?** Do you have special parts of your website dedicated to alumni of color's interests? Do you have special brochures or publications that depict the alumni of color's experiences? How do alumni of color factor into the mainstream publications?

8. **In the last 15 years, have there been any racial incidents on your campus?** Does the development staff discuss them? How do you communicate the institution's response to racial incidents to alumni of color? How do you work with the university to rectify the situation in the eyes of alumni of color?

Answering these questions is essential to moving forward in terms of engaging and soliciting alumni of color at your institution. All but a few institutions of higher education over-look alumni of color. However, we are starting to see a slight shift, more so at majority institutions where the country's demographic predictions are beginning to manifest themselves on campus. Educational powerhouses like Brown University, Cornell University, the University of Pennsylvania, Emory University and the University of North Carolina, Chapel Hill are all experiencing record numbers of students of color among their incoming classes. Gone are the days of historically White institutions with 100 percent White populations. These changes translate into alumni that are now, and will continue to become, more racially and ethnically diverse. At some point, hopefully, majority institutions will see the economic potential of this neglected segment of the population.

TALKING ABOUT RACE

Talking about race is often difficult: discussions get heated, people are often misunderstood, others do not want to be blamed or to be called racist, many are defensive, always keeping their guard up. We have found that when people are honest, patient and do not take themselves too seriously, they tend to learn more and racial barriers come down.

We often give talks in front of largely White audiences – audiences of fundraisers. We talk very frankly and openly about race and it sometimes makes people feel just a little uncomfortable at first. In fact, one development officer once approached us after a talk and said, "I didn't even know Nelson was Black until you pointed it out." He was trying hard to be colorblind – something that he had been taught as a way to avoid racist behavior. Unfortunately, being colorblind does not help anyone and in fact, can hurt relationships. It is important to recognize who someone is and to engage his or her cultural heritage. However, we do not want to judge them based only on that cultural heritage. Race is complicated but learning more about other cultures and their traditions can make us more informed and open-minded.

We are very comfortable talking about race. Part of our attitude stems from our friendship that has developed over the years. After meeting in 2006 at a fundraising conference, we struck up a friendship that began by talking – often about racial differences – and eventually led to a working partnership. Because we decided early on to be open, frank, and to never be afraid to ask questions of each other, our partnership and friendship has flourished. We encourage you to establish relationships with others who are outside your friend circle. These relationships will prove beneficial to you personally and professionally.

CHAPTER OVERVIEW

Chapter 2: African American Philanthropy and Alumni: "Uplifting the Race"

This chapter will provide an overview of the history and tradition of philanthropy among African American cultures, paying particular attention to Black alumni. We will focus on why and where Blacks give, and what fundraisers specifically need to know in order to work with and approach Black donors.

Chapter 3: Asian American and Pacific Islander Philanthropy and Alumni: "Respect and Prestige"

In this chapter, we will examine the philosophies of giving among various Asian Americans and Pacific Islander (AAPI) communities. We will also discuss giving trends and patterns, with a focus on AAPI alumni giving. The chapter provides concrete suggestions for approaching AAPI alumni.

Chapter 4: Latino Philanthropy and Alumni: "Elevating Culture and Family"

This chapter discusses philanthropy and fundraising within Latino cultures, alluding to generational and ethnic subgroup differences. The history of philanthropy among Latinos is deeply rooted in their culture and offers clues for modern-day fundraising. We will discuss trends and giving patterns and include best practices for cultivating and soliciting Latino alumni.

Chapter 5: Native American Philanthropy and Alumni: "Community over Individual"

In this chapter, we explore the philosophy of giving among Native Americans, focusing on the rich culture of circular giving, honor, and selflessness. We will discuss Native American motivations for giving, giving trends, and other issues of particular concern. Although rooted in a larger discussion of culture, we will hone in on practical ideas for how to engage and cultivate Native American alumni.

Chapter 6: A Conversation with Advancement Staff at Majority Institutions

In this chapter, we draw from the interviews we conducted with AAU institution development and alumni relations staff members. We provide examples of best practices and give you an understanding of the current landscape in terms of programs, strategies, and policies regarding engaging and soliciting alumni of color.

Chapter 7: A Conversation with Alumni of Color

Chapter 7 captures the voices of alumni of color. Through surveys we provide the perspective of alumni of color on engagement and solicitation, offering one of the first glimpses into their motivations and concerns for and about giving.

Chapter 8: Model Programs for Alumni of Color

This chapter focuses on those programs at majority institutions that serve alumni of color. We looked across institutional types for programs that could be replicated at like institutions. These programs have had much success and need to be adopted by more colleges and universities.

Chapter 9: Mistakes to Avoid

This chapter draws from the previous chapters and cuts across the various racial and ethnic groups to provide best practices that speak to alumni of color in general. We will highlight the work of model development programs, discuss how to enlist alumni of color in the fundraising process and how to capitalize on positive relationships with cultural centers and student groups on campus. In this chapter, we also urge fundraisers to move away from conventional views of fundraising, which operate from a White point of view only. We will identify common mistakes that are often alienating to alumni of color.

Chapter 10: Best Practices and Concluding Thoughts

Our concluding chapter highlights the main ideas and best practices of the book and makes recommendations for future practice.

Appendices

Although this book is a practical guide, it is research based. As such, we share the interview questions, surveys, and list of participating institutions on which we base our assertions.

Supplementary Bibliography

The book includes an expanded bibliography that can be used by scholars and practitioners alike to bolster their knowledge of philanthropy in communities of color.

2

AFRICAN AMERICAN PHILANTHROPY AND ALUMNI

"Uplifting the Race"

A long, lasting legacy of benevolence, absent need for further evidence.
Forget the twisted myths. We have always given our gifts.

Ava Woods, 2011

Since the passing of the 1964 Civil Rights Act, African Americans have had an increased presence on historically White college and university campuses. In fact, between 1984 and 2009, there has been a 240 percent increase in the number of African American students on majority campuses (National Center for Education Statistics, 2012). Yet, college fundraisers tend to ignore these students once they become alumni in terms of engagement and solicitation. Too often Blacks are seen as recipients of philanthropy rather than givers – even college-educated African Americans are ignored (Gasman & Bowman, 2011). In this chapter, we highlight the prevailing literature on Black giving, including historical and current giving patterns, while also suggesting practical strategies for increasing giving among African Americans.

WEALTH AND ASSETS

Disparities in income and assets between Blacks and Whites still remain. According to Conley (2008), "In 2007, the median White family held assets worth more than fifteen times those of the median Black family" (p. 5). For example, at the lower end of the income spectrum (less than $21,000 per year), the median African American family has no assets, while the equivalent White family holds $8,000 worth of equity. And among the top income quintile (greater than $95,000 per year), White families enjoy a median net worth of over $395,000, more than three times the figure for upper-income African American families ($109,151) (Conley, 2008). An important point to understand when talking about African American wealth is the difference between income and wealth (Edmondson & Carroll, 1999). In recent years, the income gap has been shrinking between African Americans and Whites, but the wealth divide continues to grow. Income is primarily the compensation one receives from work or the payout received from government benefits. Wealth may include income, but it is more the nature by which the income is derived (that is, real estate, savings, and stocks). Conley (2008) also notes that since wealth accumulation depends heavily on intergenerational support issues such as gifts, informal loans, and inheritances, net worth has the ability to pick up both the current dynamics of race and the legacy of past inequalities that may be obscured in simple measures of income, occupation, or education. Regardless of these disparities, African Americans have increased access to wealth. In 2009, for example, Blacks had $900 billion in buying power and that number is expected to grow substantially by 2015 due to trends in education and the rising numbers of African American women in the workforce (Nielsen Report, 2011; Selig Center for Economic Growth, 2009). This buying power can be tapped, but only if colleges and universities are ready, educated about African American giving, and ask (Kasper et al., 2004).

In addition, African American stock market participation has risen 30 percent in recent years, while home ownership is at an all time high of 48 percent, representing a 14 percent increase between 2000 and 2010 (Neilsen Report, 2011). Although African Americans have lower incomes and fewer assets, they save at the same rates as their White counterparts. In addition, African Americans have a higher rate of self-employment than Whites, opting to create their own businesses in many instances (Conley, 2008). Of most importance, research shows that despite the widening wealth gap, African Americans are just as likely as Whites to make charitable contributions and give more of their discretionary income to charity (Duran, 2001).

Given that African American wealth is not at the level of Whites, one could think that this group does not warrant significant fundraising cultivation. However, we urge the reader to think twice before making this assumption. Although current buying power for African Americans is at $900 billion, by 2015 this number will be $1.1 trillion. This level of buying power ranks African Americans as the 16th largest country in the world if comparing the buying power to Gross Domestic Product (Nielsen, 2011). African Americans have the potential to give substantially. The main reason that individuals do not give is that they are not asked. In the case of African Americans this is entirely too true. As noted, the assumption on the part of most fundraisers is that Blacks do not give philanthropically.

PHILOSOPHY OF AFRICAN AMERICAN PHILANTHROPY

According to the National Center for Black Philanthropy, within African American communities, philanthropy is based on communal notions of giving. More specifically, when individuals in Black communities support others, the entire community benefits and not just the immediate recipients of the philanthropy. This kind of caring for and sharing with one another often includes assorted gifts of time, talent, knowledge, and treasure. Research shows that these instincts stem from African Americans' lack of access to social services and the fact that they had much more time and talent to offer than treasure. In many cases, while having to battle the numerous social injustices of the time, such as slavery, lynching, and discrimination, African Americans found themselves providing charity for those less fortunate. According to Pettey (2001), "*Homo communalis*, the idea that we live and have our being in a caring society, is at the heart of African metaphysics . . . This cosmology of connectedness provided the first principle of early black philanthropy" (p. 1).

As a result of this insular and often non-financial style of philanthropy, attempts to a measure the depth and variety of African American philanthropy using traditional methods will, in many cases, provide a false reading, as their love of humanity and support of mankind will not register. Valaida Fullwood, author of *Giving Back: A Tribute to African American Philanthropy*, recently reiterated that by stating "We also give in a lot of ways that researchers don't collect data on, like when we help cover tuition for a cousin or help to pay someone's rent" (Fullwood, 2011, p. 2).

EARLY AFRICAN AMERICAN PHILANTHROPY

African American philanthropy began in the 1600s when free Blacks in the North set up self-help circles to organize their communities and fight against slavery in the South. Blacks were focused on harnessing volunteerism for the greater good and because, even in the North, they were shut out from most social services offered by communities and churches, they had to provide for each other as a people (Gasman & Sedgwick, 2005). In the South, under the horrors of slavery, African Americans were also giving to one another. For example, in her beautifully written book *Self-Taught*, Heather Williams discusses how Blacks taught each other to read in order to better the race despite the fact that learning to read and teaching someone to read was illegal in all Southern states (Wallenstein, 2008). According to Pettey (2001), "The majority of enslaved Africans lived in conditions that were deplorable. These conditions led them to develop survival skills and other means of helping one another, using whatever limited resources they had available" (p. 5).

By the 1700s, Black philanthropy started to take shape as formal mutual aid societies from the Underground Railroad to civil rights organizations (Gasman & Sedgwick, 2005). According to Duran (2001), mutual aid organizations worked diligently to abolish slavery. In fact, they were so effective that "several states established laws to ban fraternal organizations and mutual aid societies" (p. 4). Those Blacks that supported the Underground Railroad also participated in fundraising campaigns to raise money for the movement. Many of these organizations were affiliated with or coordinated through churches; others were affiliated with fraternal organizations such as the Prince Hall Masons (Copeland-Carson, 2005; Jacobs, 1988). Because African Americans had little to give in terms of tangible goods, volunteerism was an important aspect of Black giving (Copeland-Carson, 2005). Moreover, most giving was in response to an immediate need; it was crisis driven. Eventually these mutual aid groups led to the creation of such organizations as the National Urban League and the United Negro

College Fund – organizations dedicated to raising money for and empowering African American communities (Gasman, 2007; Gasman & Sedgwick, 2005).

By the 1800s, the Black church was very active in the North, especially in cities like Philadelphia and New York. Churches such as the African Methodist Episcopal Church and the African Methodist Episcopal Zion Church were instrumental in providing services, goods, and counsel to Blacks throughout the North (Copeland-Carson, 2005; Gasman & Bowman, 2011; Gasman & Sedgwick, 2005). In addition, after the Civil War, these churches sent missionaries South to educate former slaves (Anderson, 1988). Most of these missionaries taught at historically Black colleges and universities or makeshift primary schools. In many cases these small Black colleges refused to take monies from White philanthropists and only relied on the philanthropy and volunteerism of African Americans (Gasman & Drezner, 2009, 2011).

Also during the 1800s, Black fraternities and sororities were created (Gasman, 2005, 2011a; Gasman, Louison, & Barnes, 2008). These organizations, although initially social in nature, began to provide services to Black communities. According to Pettey (2001), "There is considerable evidence that students at Cornell University, who formed the Alpha Phi Alpha [Fraternity], were seriously concerned about the negative conditions affecting Blacks" (p. 7). Historian Paula Giddings (2007), who is also a member of Delta Sigma Theta Sorority, notes that the Deltas and other sororities' efforts included mobile libraries, civil rights advocacy, voter education, and leadership training for youth. They also raised substantial scholarship funds for students to attend college (Gasman, 2005; Gasman & Sedgwick, 2005).

The mid-1900s saw the rise of civil rights-oriented philanthropy (Garrow, 1987). Not only did Black churches raise money and fund civil rights activities, but individual African Americans banded together to support civil rights leaders, including students at the nation's Black colleges. For example, Black citizens of Greensboro, North Carolina, came together to support the Bennett College for Women and North Carolina A&T University students in their fight to desegregate eating establishments in the area (Chafe, 1981; Gasman, 2011b).

Today, there is an emphasis on bringing together funds in an organized way in the form of family foundations (Gasman, 2010). Many African Americans do not trust banks and other formal organizations. As such, they are less likely to deposit their funds in community foundations and instead have chosen to establish family foundations aimed at making changes in education and health care. These foundations range in assets from $425,000 to $40,000,000 (Gasman, 2010).

MOTIVATIONS FOR BLACK GIVING

African Americans often give in small increments (Gasman & Anderson-Thompkins, 2003). The main reason for this strategy is that there is a lack of trust around giving to mainstream organizations due to past injustices (Gasman & Bowman, 2011). Blacks typically give in small amounts at first and then increase their giving as they become more comfortable with an institution. Among more affluent African Americans, it is typical to give in larger amounts (Carson, 1993c; W. K. Kellogg Foundation, 2012).

Although receiving a tax deduction is not the main reason why White Americans give philanthropically, it is one reason and plays a significant role (Giving USA, 2010). Moreover, Whites, by and large, deduct charitable giving on their tax returns. Among African American first-time donors, especially those who are low or middle income, earning a tax deduction is not of importance. In fact, in terms of church-related giving, many African Americans consider it wrong to receive something in exchange for their giving (Gasman & Bowman, 2011). For example, consider the following story about Nelson's mother:

> After my mother's death in 2008, I had the opportunity to comb through her papers and came across her annual giving statements to the church. One year she gave $2,300, another year $3,000 and then the largest amount of all $4,500. The uniqueness of this – my mother never made more than $21,000 a year so those charitable gifts to the church represented roughly 11 to 22 percent of her annual income. Researching a bit more, I discovered two things about my mother. First, her other charitable gifts to other organizations within a given year never exceeded $1,000 and, secondly, her tax returns throughout the years never reflected any deductions for the donations.

This example supports research that shows that within African American households, tax benefits are not as important. In fact, they are even less important to Black women than they are to Black men. Black women are typically the philanthropic arm of the family, making these decisions. Moreover, women tend to be more involved in the church, including the choir, mission societies and usher boards and, as a result, they feel more strongly about tithing and giving back (Lincoln & Mamiya, 1990).

One of the main reasons that African Americans give is that they have a commitment – almost a sense of obligation – to racial uplift (Carson, 1993c; Gasman & Anderson-Thompkins, 2003). Black alumni, specifically, want to provide the same opportunities to future generations that were provided to them. Oftentimes, Black alumni will use the phrase, "reach back and pull someone up," referring to their commitment to racial uplift (Gasman & Anderson-Thompkins, 2003). For centuries, African Americans had to rely on only themselves to make change in Black communities and this sense of commitment has not changed despite the end of legalized segregation and the progress of integration (Wallenstein, 2008).

As mentioned earlier, trust is a key issue with regard to giving among African Americans. Because Blacks were mistreated and taken advantage of by mainstream organizations such as banks and the legal enterprise, they are less inclined to trust initially if unfamiliar with an organization (Gasman & Sedgwick, 2005). Trust is essential in all giving situations but for Blacks extra time and effort needs to be invested in order to put donors at ease.

African Americans, especially newer givers, prefer to give to more concrete causes. They prefer to give to causes that they can see and touch, such as scholarships or building funds (Gasman & Bowman, 2011). Because of their inclination to give to concrete causes, it tends to be difficult to convince Blacks to give to endowment campaigns. This type of giving is nebulous and often needs to be explained. By and large, most alumni in general do not understand how endowment giving works. One of the best approaches to explaining endowments with any audience, but especially with first-time, African American givers, is to compare an endowment to a savings account. We recommend discussing gifts to the operating budget as putting money in the checking account and giving to the endowment as putting money in a savings account. The endowment sustains the institution like savings sustain a family during difficult financial times (Gasman & Bowman, 2011).

African Americans are also motivated to give by their peers and family (Gasman & Anderson-Thompkins, 2003). Because of this influence, giving circles or giving within social organizations is particularly successful. For example, giving challenges among Black alumni who are close friends (or were in college) are often successful as there is a healthy amount of competition among these alumni (Gasman & Anderson-Thompkins, 2003). In addition, giving that takes advantage of fraternity or sorority membership is often quite successful because of the fraternal bonds established among members of these organizations. There is a sense of positive peer pressure among these organizations that can be used as the impetus for giving on a regular basis (Gasman & Anderson-Thompkins, 2003; Gasman et al., 2008).

WHERE BLACKS GIVE AND WHY

There are five major areas to which African Americans give philanthropically: emergency assistance, religion, education, civil rights, and health-related issues (Copeland-Carson, 2005; Gasman & Bowman, 2011). All of these issues touch Blacks personally and, as a result, they are close to their hearts and minds. First, Blacks give to their family and friends in cases of emergency. As many Blacks have had limited access to quality health care and good nutrition over the years, family members often come to the rescue of each other when in need. In the words of Pettey (2001), "Although some may criticize spontaneous giving, let us remember that it has been an important way for blacks of all socioeconomic levels to give back" (p. 9).

Among all racial and ethnic groups, religion is the largest recipient of charitable giving (Giving USA, 2010; Steinberg & Wilhelm, 2005). However, for most African Americans, the Black church has been a one-stop shop for generation after generation, providing faith, education, entertainment, and social networking needs (Gasman & Bowman, 2011; Holloman, Gasman, & Anderson-Thompkins, 2003; Lincoln & Mamiya, 1990). The church provided social services when the government and communities excluded Blacks (Lincoln & Mamiya, 1990). Due to this close and influential relationship, African Americans are very likely to give to the church and in fact, give 60 percent of their philanthropic dollars to churches across the nation (Gasman & Bowman, 2011). According to Pettey (2001), "The black church is historically the main recipient of black philanthropy and the catalyst for social, civic, educational, and economic action, as well as the center for religious activity. It is the institution that has been traditionally owned and controlled by blacks. Ownership and control are the elements of trust that result in the strong financial support for these churches" (p. 10).

Another area that is particularly important in terms of African American giving is education. Blacks see education as a necessity to advancement in society and as such it is concrete in nature. Blacks tend to give to concrete causes such as scholarships. In fact, at times, within the education setting, African Americans will only give to scholarships as they see this type of giving as tangible (Gasman & Anderson-Thompkins, 2003). The monies go to a specific cause or student and the giver knows that a check was issued.

African Americans have long supported civil rights causes as mentioned above and they continue to do so today. Because racism is still a viable problem in the United States, there continues to be civil rights issues and social causes that have an impact on the daily lives and rights of Blacks. In recent years, Blacks have rallied around issues such as unfair treatment in the judicial and criminal justice systems and education, in particular. African Americans are heavily inclined to give to civil rights initiatives that are closely tied to their communities (Gasman & Bowman, 2011; Gasman & Sedgwick, 2005).

The last area to which African Americans pay particular attention is health. They tend to focus on those health-related issues that affect Black communities the most, such as high blood pressure, diabetes, heart disease, HIV/AIDS, and the disease that Blacks hold the exclusive rights on – sickle cell anemia (Gasman & Bowman, 2011). Because so many family members suffer from these diseases, Blacks are likely to give to both research and practice related to these health issues (W. K. Kellogg Foundation, 2012).

BEST APPROACHES TO ENGAGING AND SOLICITING AFRICAN AMERICAN ALUMNI

Research noting the motivations for giving among African Americans is important, but being able to apply that research to methods of engagement and solicitation is vital. The most successful fundraising appeals are those tied to racial uplift.

These appeals are powerful among Black donors overall and Black alumni specifically. When asking for institutional support, it is important to show donors how their contribution will have an impact on the lives of African Americans. It is also important to include messages of racial uplift, obligation, and giving back in publications and solicitations that go to African American alumni. Black alumni respond to these kinds of messages.

A second effective strategy to fundraising among African American alumni is to use personal approaches. Of course, we all try to do this as often as possible in fundraising, but it is absolutely essential when working with Black donors. Direct mail is typically not successful with Black alumni, especially at majority institutions that lack diversity. All too often, these institutions distribute fundraising pieces that only represent the majority students. African American alumni want to see people who look like them in publications. They also want to be engaged by individuals, not paper. Using one-on-one approaches, in which the fundraiser or alumni staff member is familiar with the alumnus' background, take time but it is much more effective.

Having a specific contact in the fundraising and alumni relations offices with which African American alumni can become familiar is important. That is not to say that everyone in the development office is not responsible for all alumni and donors – we think they are – but having dedicated staff is important as well. Our research shows that the institutions with dedicated staff members are more engaged around Black giving overall, keeping track of it, having special affinity groups, and drawing from the Black alumni for leadership positions.

A third effective approach to fundraising includes working with clergy members directly. Within Black communities, clergy are incredibly influential and persuasive. Working with local churches to encourage African American giving can be fruitful. Regardless of institutional type, including public or private status, this is an important strategy and is rarely done on a regular basis. In making presentations to churches, majority institutions needs to show the congregants what they can do for the local Black community and the institution's track record of reaching out beyond the borders of the campus. Establishing relationships with local alumni involved in the church can be quite fruitful and result in the creation of scholarship programs that churches match. Not only do these university–church relationships help raise funds, but they also help build a stronger reputation in the local Black community and help to increase the number of African American student applicants to an institution's degree programs.

A fourth approach to fundraising is establishing trust among donors. We noted above that trust is one of the main motivators for Black giving. Majority institutions need to work hard to establish trust. Based on their experiences, many Black alumni have a tremendous lack of trust in their alma mater. It is vital that majority institutions invest in rebuilding trust and it is essential to emphasize the changes that are being implemented at the institution – changes that will make the place better for future African American students. Black alumni and donors want to know that their donations are being spent on positive change and programs that will benefit African Americans.

A fifth approach is collaboration with those involved in African American sororities and fraternities (alumni who are involved in local chapters); also those alumni involved in social groups – such as the Links, Jack and Jill, 100 Black Men, and the Boule. African Americans respond to personal solicitations as noted earlier. Linking fundraising to these social organizations results in fundraising based on personal relationships. Too often these social organizations are not tapped into in meaningful ways. The women and men in these social organizations give ample time and money to various causes around the country, and higher education has been and should continue to be one of these causes. Of course, the problem at many majority institutions is that the development staff is overwhelmingly White and, as such, is often unfamiliar with these African American organizations. This is why it is essential that development staff members participate in professional development sessions related to fundraising in diverse communities and that they familiarize themselves with the resources available on the topic. Of note, leaders in offices of development and alumni relations need to require their staff members to attend these sessions on diverse communities because most people will not attend them of their own accord. The best approach is to attend as a team.

Given the history of African Americans in the United States – a history of mistreatment, unfairness, and oppression – it is important for majority colleges and universities to be sensitive to the experiences and needs of this population. Black–White race relations are perhaps the most volatile in the country and in order to engage Black alumni, development offers need to acknowledge the situation and attempt to understand it by educating themselves and others. Seeing Blacks as givers is the first step in this process.

3

ASIAN AMERICAN AND PACIFIC ISLANDER PHILANTHROPY AND ALUMNI

"Respect and Prestige"

Asian American and Pacific Islanders (AAPIs) are one of the fastest growing minority populations in the United States along with Latinos (Pew Research Center, 2012). Between the years 2000 and 2012, the population has grown by 42.9 percent and it is projected to grow another 134 percent to over 35.6 million in the next 40 years (Pew Research Center, 2012). Understanding this community is vital to the future of the United States. Of note, the AAPI community is remarkably diverse in terms of ethnicity. It is 22 percent Chinese, 19 percent Filipino, 16 percent Indian, 10 percent Vietnamese, 9 percent Korean, 6 percent Japanese, and 18 percent other (including those who are Pakistani, Cambodian, Hmong, Thai, Laotian, Taiwanese, Bangladeshi, Burmese, Indonesian, Nepalese, Sri Lankan, Malaysian, Native Hawaiian, Samoan, and Bhutanese).

As the AAPI community grows, it is also acquiring substantial wealth. In 2002 and 2004, for example, more AAPIs contributed (or possessed) to their 401K & Savings Plan than any other racial group. Likewise, in 2002 and 2004, AAPIs possessed more interest-earning assets at financial institutions across all racial groups. In terms of business ownership, among people of color, AAPIs possess the most and the highest value of financial loans. And while each ethnicity group experienced growth in acquiring business loans between the years of 1990 and 2000, only the AAPI population continued that growth through 2010. For the other groups there was an average decline in business loans of more than 19 percent.

AAPIs are the least likely, along with Whites, to be uninsured in the United States. And, with the exception of Whites, AAPIs are more likely to own Money Market Deposit Accounts (16 percent). Moreover, AAPIs are the most likely among racial and ethnic minorities to have interest-earning checking accounts. However, when these statistics are disaggregated, it becomes apparent that there is great disparity across the various AAPI ethnic groups (Commission on Research on Asian American and Pacific Islander Research in Education, 2011).

PHILOSOPHY OF ASIAN AMERICAN AND PACIFIC ISLANDER PHILANTHROPY

The AAPI culture of giving is based on commonly held beliefs in the value of compassion, the importance of relationships with family, and the reciprocity of gift-giving (Tokumura, 2001). Philanthropic traditions within AAPI communities are also heavily influenced by cultural traditions, religion, and generational patterns. The major AAPI religions, including Buddhism, Taoism, Islam, Confucianism, Hinduism, and Catholicism, play a significant role in establishing a philanthropic foundation and the subsequent habits of AAPIs. According to Pettey (2001), "The teachings of Buddha emphasize compassion and service to others; from Confucius comes benevolence and piety" (p. 21). In addition, Confucian notions of giving promote the idea that giving should be done quietly so as not to draw attention to oneself and so as not to "extract personal benefit from altruism" (Tsunoda, 2010, p. 7). Lao Tzu teaches the relatedness of all things, and the reciprocity that characterizes all human relationships. The underlying values of Sikhism, practiced by many Indians from the Punjab region, stress sharing with those in need and giving time to charity.

Among AAPIs, giving is linked to family and one's social circles and these circles expand as individuals increase their income. As people secure more financial means, their giving moves from survival- and emergency-related giving to "quality of life" giving (Chao, 1999). One of the main components of AAPI giving is annual remittance, estimated to be in the billions (Chao, 1999; Pettey, 2002; Yin, 2004). For example, Filipino Americans remit up to $6.4 billion each year, Bangladeshis $1.6 billion, and Vietnamese-Americans $500 million annually (Duran, 2001). Moreover, as AAPIs become more assimilated they are more likely to give to social justice and civil rights causes. In addition, their sense of obligation to philanthropic giving grows. They see it as essential to civic engagement and political participation (Chao, 1999). AAPIs are also more likely to give to mainstream nonprofits as they become more assimilated. And, once they begin to give financial contributions, they typically begin to volunteer, serve on boards and event related committees (Chao, 1999; Yin, 2004). The first nonprofit to which AAPIs give is typically the United Way, but once donors become more acquainted with the diversity of the nonprofit community, the United Way does not necessarily remain the top recipient of funds (Chao, 1999; Duran, 2001). According to Duran (2001), "Studies have also consistently found that Asians can be characterized as 'substantial givers,' giving more than 2.5% of their household income to charity" (p. 37).

GIVING PATTERNS BY ETHNIC GROUP

There is incredible diversity among the various AAPI ethnic groups (Commission on Research on Asian American and Pacific Islander Research in Education, 2011). With that in mind, we are providing information on the different segments of the population. In addition, it is important to note that giving changes among all racial and ethnic groups as people become more assimilated into mainstream culture. In particular, in AAPI groups, generational status and the length of time a person has been in the United States matters. Wealth and accumulation of wealth also makes a significant difference in giving among AAPI populations as well (Yin, 2004).

Chinese

Philanthropy in Chinese culture starts from birth. For example, when a baby is one month old her parents host a red egg and ginger banquet to celebrate the birth. As part of this tradition, it is customary for guests to make contributions to their favorite philanthropies in honor of the baby and her parents (Pettey, 2001). Within Chinese culture, there is a tradition referred to as *Yeuhng ga*, which means the shared responsibility to care for families. This tradition manifests here in the United States in the form of sending money back to families in China. Another Chinese concept that is linked to philanthropy is *Heung yajh gam*, which is similar in nature to *Yeuhng ga* but focused more on school building. This tradition encourages Chinese people to provide funding to schools and youth education (Yin, 2004). Another Chinese concept that is particularly important and empowering is *Bong*, which refers to giving both financial and in-kind giving to new immigrants who are struggling to make it in the United States. Although giving under the auspices of *Bong* is typically to family members or local community members, sometimes this concept is extended to strangers (Osili & Du

2005; Yin, 2004). Philanthropy within Chinese culture also extends into a person's life cycle. For example, when individuals turn 50, they are celebrated with the announcement of public donations to organizations that are meaningful to the person being celebrated. This concept is call *Daaih Sang yaht*. Many Chinese traditions are linked to philanthropic giving. And reciprocity is central to the acts of giving within Chinese communities (Yin, 2004).

Filipino

Another ethnic group within AAPI culture is Filipinos. Filipino philanthropy is based on familial support and a sense of obligation and responsibility to one's extended family. In addition, Catholicism has played a substantial part in the giving traditions of Filipinos. Most of the philanthropy among Filipinos pertains to family and family ties. For example, a child's godparents are expected to give financially throughout a child's life and support his well-being. Furthermore, Filipinos have a term for donations related to religion-based giving – *Abuloy*. This type of philanthropy is common when someone dies as relatives and friends give to the deceased's family to defray funeral costs. Like the Chinese, Filipinos also send money back to those living in their homeland. They feel obligated to support those living in the villages and neighborhoods from which they hail. And for those individuals and families arriving from the Philippines, people already in the United States help out immediately, giving to those in need. Of note, this kind of giving is not always in the form of money, but is often food or lodging. An interesting caveat about Filipino philanthropy is that due to the strong familial ties, outside support is sometimes considered nonessential. Families are tight-knit and rather than branching out to meet new people, they tend to live near each other and socialize together (Pettey, 2001).

Koreans

There are roughly 1.5 million Korean Americans living in the United States. Of note, one in every three Korean Americans was born here. In 1960 there were only 11,000 Koreans in the United States. This AAPI ethic group is growing rapidly. This growth, attributed to birth rates in the United States, is advantageous for philanthropy because most of these individuals are upwardly mobile and also tend to come from more Americanized families that are willing and interested in participating in mainstream philanthropy (Give2Asia, 2010). Of note, those Koreans who immigrated to the United States were well-educated and also had professional backgrounds, which makes them different from many other immigrants (Osili & Du, 2005). They are more likely to acquire wealth and stature and give in larger amounts (Give2Asia, 2010).

Much like other AAPI groups, Koreans begin with informal giving and typically give in relation to births, weddings, and deaths. However, once they become more assimilated, they move away from this kind of giving or add to it (Give2Asia, 2010). Koreans also give substantially to churches, mainly those that are Christian. Of note, philanthropic giving to the church tends to be inward-looking if the church is made up of immigrant families (Osili & Du, 2005). As Koreans become more affluent and assimilate into American culture, they continue to give to the church but their giving and that of their churches tends to be more outward in nature, focusing on the community and uplifting it (Give2Asia, 2010).

Japanese

The underlying premise of giving among the Japanese can be traced to the influence of both Buddhist and Confucian religions in Japan (Onishi, 2007). According to Duran (2001), "Religious teachings of compassion, service to others and the relatedness of all things make giving . . . integral to everyday life; philanthropy as such, is not considered a separate activity" (p. 26). Unlike many other AAPI cultures, the purpose of giving among Japanese people is motivated by a desire for harmony among people and with nature. This is distinctly different from many other AAPIs as well as other racial and ethnic groups. Japanese Americans are also shaped in their philanthropic giving by the United States' history of oppression during World War II, remembering their own internment or that of their family members (Onishi, 2007).

Much like African Americans, Japanese donors like to see results from their giving and enjoy celebrating the success that results from giving. They often give money to family and community members for luck and celebrate the results of this luck later in life. Like other AAPI groups, the Japanese give money for sympathy. They refer to this giving as *Omimai* and with the act of giving money the giver is demonstrating care and concern for others. In more recent years, given all of the floods, earthquakes, and other natural disasters happening in AAPI countries, *Omimai* has been given to sympathize with those going through these events. The Japanese also give money to the deceased's family to pay for funeral costs and those costs associated with moving to a new place in life. This type of giving is referred to as *Koden* (Onishi, 2007).

The Japanese are quite advanced in terms of philanthropy and fundraising. According to Onishi (2007), "the source of Japanese charitable organizations can be traced back to *Shiki-in* built by Prince Shotoku during the seventh century" (Onishi, 2007). *Kanjin*, a Japanese Buddhist model of organized fundraising, dates from the eighth century and developed during the eleventh century. *Kanjin* resembles today's capital campaign because it was organized to raise funds for a specific project, such as building a temple, and people were solicited according to their financial capability (p. 33). Philanthropy was a long-held tradition in Japan until after World War II. At that point, the nation's Constitution was revised and giving declined. Today, some Japanese individuals are now somewhat resistant to hardcore fundraising and feel that it is a forceful act. Oftentimes, the term fundraising is offensive within Japanese culture, especially when used aggressively.

More than any other AAPI ethnic group, the Japanese often give to civil rights, civil liberties, and political representation causes. Although much of this giving is focused on the Japanese American community, the Japanese will also give to mainstream organizations that focus on these types of issues. Perhaps this support of civil rights and civil liberties is linked to the treatment of the Japanese people here in the United States during World War II (Chao, 1999).

According to Onishi (2007), Japanese philanthropy is shaped by a strong sense of etiquette, respect for elders, and an orientation toward the larger group over the individual. More specifically, "the Japanese are more likely to support individuals, organizations, or communities they know in person, especially if asked by respected persons or family" (p. 37).

Indians

Philanthropy is deeply rooted in Indian culture and is based on thousands of years of tradition. According to a recent report by the Silicon Valley Community Foundation, "The importance of giving back to the community through civic engagement, donations, and volunteerism has been codified in ancient religions, spread by Mahatma Gandhi's movement for the social transformation, and compelled by India's growing presence on the world stage" (p. 3). Much of the focus on philanthropy in Indian culture is tied to religion, including Hinduism, Buddhism, and Islam (Anand, 2003). Unselfish giving is a major tenet of the ancient Hindu texts. For example, religious texts speak about one's *dharma* (religious obligations) as being their *daan* (moral duties). Giving can be financial, in kind, or through volunteerism but it must be done without the expectation of a reward. According to the Silicon Valley Community Foundation report, "Giving for Indians has traditionally been a personal and private undertaking, focused on family, caste, community and village" (2012, p. 3). In the United States, Indian Americans typically give to causes that support their homeland of India as well as causes that assist Indian populations here in the United States. In addition, they are generous toward the communities in which they live (Silicon Valley Community Foundation, 2012). Indians care most about education and youth programs, then health related giving, and then arts and culture. The majority of Indian giving in the United States is in these three areas (Anand, 2003). Faith-based giving is important but it differs depending on the level of assimilation, generational status, and belief in God (some Indians adhere to the cultural aspects of a religion but not the spiritual aspects) (Silicon Valley Community Foundation, 2012). Of note, Indians see philanthropy as an investment in their future in the United States.

Native Hawaiians

Native Hawaiians are those individuals with traceable lineage to the Hawaiian Islands prior to Western contact in 1778. According to Rothwell (2011), "the tumultuous history of colonization, shift to capitalism and away from traditional economic and governance systems, and most recently globalization explain why Native Hawaiians are socio-economically disadvantaged and marginalized today" (p. 40). In fact, the rate of Native Hawaiian poverty is now double the state's average, 15 percent compared to 7.1 percent (Naya, 2007). In addition, Native Hawaiians disproportionately fill low status jobs and own homes that are only two-thirds the value of those of non-Native Hawaiians in

Hawaii. Native Hawaiians' low wages and lack of assets combined with high rates of poverty have a negative impact on their social outcomes (Rothwell, 2011).

Due to high instances of poverty, Native Hawaiians have not participated fully in formal philanthropy. However, they are intensely generous with their family and friends, assisting with community needs. Because Native Hawaiians feel a deep connection to the land from which they sprung, they are interested in giving to environmental causes and to efforts to preserve the Hawaiian land and culture. They feel that the land around them gives them their sense of "love, joy, and nourishment" (Aluli-Meyer, 2008). Native Hawaiians also support programs aimed at enhancing self-sufficiency and self-determination (Rothwell, 2011). Being part of the political process is a natural part of Native Hawaiian life and is deeply respected and encouraged.

When approaching Native Hawaiians within the fundraising context, it is important to do so in a respectful way – a way in which cultural values and traditions are held up high. Imposing Western traditions and values on Native Hawaiians tends to discourage philanthropic giving. The giving must include native traditions.

MOTIVATION FOR AAPI GIVING

There are several main reasons why AAPIs give. The first is to help friends and family and this motivation permeates all AAPI ethnic groups. Among immigrant groups, it is very common to support family and friends because there is great need, especially when these kin are new to the country (Osili & Du, 2005).

Positive personal connections are an important motivator for giving. According to Tsunoda (2010), "This people-to-people interaction develops the trust and respect between the organization and donors as well as the recipients" (p. 7). Chinese donors, in particular, value personal relationships as they support networking and interdependence over individuality. In fact, "personal relationships and connections tend to carry more weight than formal, institutional, contractual or legal relationships" (Tsunoda, 2010, p. 7).

As mentioned above, AAPIs often send money to their home country. They are deeply motivated to support those they left to come to the United States as well as those schools and programs in their homeland that aim to educate their relatives.

Another motivation for giving includes a desire to support AAPI rituals and institutions (Yin, 2004). These rituals and institutions are often tied to churches and temples but can also be linked to ethnic heritage. This type of motivation stems from a need to promote better understanding of AAPI history and culture as well. For example, five years ago, a Chinese philanthropist named Tang made a large gift to the Metropolitan Museum of Art in New York City. His donation, which is estimated to be roughly $14 million, enabled the museum to purchase 11 major paintings from art collector C. C. Wang, and subsequently pushed the museum to the forefront of Chinese art.

WHERE AAPIS GIVE AND WHY

Although we have given some indication of the areas for potential giving within AAPI communities overall and within the various ethnic groups, here we dig a bit deeper, providing more specifics. In general, larger gifts among AAPIs are the result of three major factors:

1. the philanthropic support was for a specific project;
2. the donor was involved with the organization prior to the gift, either serving on a board or volunteering time;
3. the contribution was made for direct services.

AAPIs tend to avoid pass-through organizations unless they are greatly assimilated (Chao, 1999).

One of the main areas for AAPI giving is education. According to research on Asian American giving, education is prized by those who believe in Confucian ideas ("Asian-American giving—the Chinese," 2002). Educational giving manifests in youth programs, at the K-12 level and within the college and university environment. Education at all levels is valued. Although one might think, given the stereotypes that result from the model minority myth, that AAPIs only give to prestigious institutions, they do not (the model minority myth refers to the idea that AAPIs do not struggle academically or financially. This has been shown to be false when AAPI data is disaggregated). There are large numbers of AAPIs living in poverty in the United States. Moreover, 50 percent of AAPIs are enrolled in community colleges (Commission on Research on Asian American and Pacific Islander Research in Education, 2011). Thus, giving is not only focused on prestigious boarding schools or Ivy League institutions, but it is also directed to the schools that have uplifted low-income AAPIs. For example, many AAPIs support "Saturday schools," which are frequented by new AAPI immigrants and often sponsored by volunteer parent groups. Nearly the entire school is built on a foundation of volunteerism and in kind giving – from teachers to facilities. As AAPIs become second and third generation Americans they are less likely to participate in "Saturday schools" (Chao, 1999). Of note, these "Saturday schools" not only benefit from philanthropy but they are also the impetus for philanthropic giving. They sponsor holiday celebrations for local communities, collect funds from the students and their families who attend them, and raise funds for victims of national disasters and emergencies (Chao, 1999).

With regard to philanthropic giving at the higher education level, many AAPIs are grateful for the opportunities that they have been given as a result of attending college. For example, according to one Japanese American, donors have a special relationship with their alma maters. This is especially true among older Japanese Americans who were often turned away by institutions that did not want to affiliate with them due to national prejudices and sentiments. Other donors saw school as a "refuge" from their own country – a way to escape the atrocities in their homeland – and they want to give back because they feel both grateful and obligated (Chao, 1999).

Another area that is greatly supported by AAPIs is service to the elderly. Among AAPI cultures, the elderly are revered and respected and people are not only willing to give in kind to help them but they give financially to support services that make life easier for elderly members of the community (W. K. Kellogg Foundation, 2012).

Perhaps one of the areas in which there is greatest philanthropic support among AAPIs is human rights (W. K. Kellogg Foundation, 2012). Many Asian countries have experienced difficulties around these issues and those AAPIs here in the United States are supportive of those in their homelands and also bringing awareness to these issues beyond their homeland's borders. Of interest, some AAPIs consider political donations to either candidates or political action committees to be philanthropic. They do not distinguish between tax deductible and non-deductible giving. In their minds, all of this giving is related to uplifting the community and participating in the many dimensions of American life (Chao, 1999). Other donors give to human rights causes that protect religious freedoms and promote gender equality.

BEST APPROACHES TO ENGAGING AND SOLICITING AAPI ALUMNI

As with most racial and ethnic groups, giving and gift size increases with greater assimilation into American culture for AAPIs. As they become more comfortable with organizations, AAPIs give more frequently and in larger amounts (W. K.

Kellogg Foundation, 2012). And, according to Chao (1999), as quoted in an article on Asian American philanthropy, all donors, especially major donors in the AAPI community, think it is important to not only be engaged, but visibly involved in organizations to which they donate ("Asian-American giving—the Chinese," 2002).

AAPIs are much more willing to give if asked by a respected member of their particular ethnic community (Smith et al., 1999). Because successful individuals as well as elders are deeply respected in AAPI cultures, it is best to involve these individuals in gift solicitations. In addition, when prominent individuals give, it serves as an impetus for their peers to give. For example, Lulu Wang, a Chinese American who leads the Tupelo Capital Management group in New York City, gave a $25 million gift to her alma mater Wellesley College. Initially, she was very quiet about her donation but Wellesley persuaded her to be vocal about the gift as it would attract other donors. According to Wang (2002), as quoted in an article on Chinese philanthropy, "It's much more comfortable to be fairly private in your philanthropy than to be a spokesman . . . We have to take some form of visible leadership" ("Asian-American giving—the Chinese," 2002, p. 3). Some AAPIs find it difficult to turn down a friend or colleague when solicited, especially if that person is highly respected in the community.

Fundraisers that work with various AAPI communities suggest drawing upon issues such as pride, family, and community when working with AAPI donors. In fact, gifts made in memory of a lost loved one are most common and tend to happen most successfully when the "ask" involves a respected individual (Chao, 1999). AAPIs also like to be associated with and give to prestigious institutions, especially those AAPIs that are more assimilated into American culture.

With AAPI donors, face time, or in-person engagement, is essential. Of course, all donors want this but with AAPI populations it leads to increased trust and the establishment of more prosperous relationships, especially when the organization is new to the donor. According to Onishi (2007), AAPIs "need to confirm feelings of 'sharing' first before being asked for donations" (p. 27) and he notes that this is frustrating to American fundraisers because they think the gift solicitation process is too time-consuming. For example, in Japanese culture it is best to avoid direct pressure when fundraising. However, once the relationship matures, face-to-face solicitations raise substantial amounts of money (Onishi, 2007, p. 28). As more and more of the population is becoming Asian, it is essential that fundraisers learn to be patient with other cultural traditions and fashion their skills to complement these cultures.

More than any other racial group, AAPIs are often lumped together and information about them is rarely disaggregated. This practice leads to misunderstandings and uninformed views of the various subgroups. Those in college and university development need to educate themselves about the specific nature of these subgroups, especially if there are significant numbers of students who belong to them on their campuses. Not knowing the differences may result in offending potential alumni donors and missed contributions and engagement.

4

LATINO PHILANTHROPY AND ALUMNI

"Elevating Culture and Family"

In the words of Danny Villanueva, "Hispanics are generous by nature, but they do not give in a vacuum. They need to be targeted and approached. It must be someone credible and culturally competent from the Latino community's perspective, who understands and can appeal to the Latino community's strong notion of family and extended family ties." Villanueva is recognized as one of the first NFL players of Hispanic descent, having played in Los Angeles and Dallas. Following his career he used football as a platform for bigger things. Today, he is a philanthropist and multimillionaire, having co-founded the Spanish language networks, Univision and Telemundo. His words are powerful as they relate to Latino philanthropy.

The Latino population in the United States is growing rapidly both through immigration and birth rates. Latinos of all ethnic backgrounds are also entering college at rapid rates and will become a dominant force among alumni in a short time. The question is whether or not colleges and universities are prepared for the changing nature of their alumni base? Do development officers and alumni relations staff members understand the complexities of Latino cultures?

Latinos make up 16.3 percent (50.5 million) of the population and 24 percent of total higher education enrollment. In the past 20 years, their wealth and influence has grown tremendously. For example, the number of Latino households with incomes over $100,000 has risen 126 percent (U.S. Census, 2010). Latinos have nearly $350 billion in buying power, an amount that has been growing at an incredible rate since the 1990s and continues to grow (Marx & Carter, 2008; Parra, 1999). In addition, 80 percent of Latinos are in the American workforce as compared to 67 percent of the nation's citizens overall. This statistic is attributed to the strong work ethic of Latinos as well as their entrepreneurial spirit. A good portion of this workforce involvement is in the area of business creation. Latino businesses have grown at a rate of three times that of the U.S. rate for business growth (Marx & Carter, 2008; Parra, 1999). With regard to philanthropic giving, 63 percent of Latino households are making charitable contributions. Volunteerism is on the rise among Latino communities as well, growing at a rate of 20 percent every five years for the past few decades (Marx & Carter, 2008; Ramos & Kasper, 2000). According to Cortés (1999), Latinos are rapidly establishing their own nonprofits to meet the needs of Latino communities. New nonprofits are being formed at a rate of 300 per year (Marx & Carter, 2008).

Given the fact that the Latino population has experienced one of the largest growth spurts of all ethnic groups within the last few years, it is somewhat surprising that major foundation support of their causes remains around 1 percent. In a 2011 report, *Foundation Funding for Hispanics/Latinos in the United*

States and for Latin America, the Foundation Center in collaboration with Hispanics in Philanthropy (HIP) highlighted many of the giving disparities associated with the funding of Latino causes by U.S. foundations (Foundation Center, 2011). Of the $41 billion directed to nonprofits between 2007 and 2009, only $206 million (0.5 percent) was directed toward Latinos and their subsequent issues. Human services and health care captured the largest shares of grant dollars receiving 27 percent and 26 percent, respectively. Recipient organizations in the Western region of the United States received the largest share (42 percent) of the donations. The vast majority of funds were donated in California, with Los Angeles garnering the most. Foundation support must increase for this population segment.

As a result of their community continuing to be largely ignored by mainstream philanthropy, Latinos have created and funded their own nonprofits to serve their communities (W. K. Kellogg Foundation, 2012). From the humble beginnings of providing cultural traditions and very informal forms of community assistance, today's Latino nonprofit organizations run as well-oiled machines. Each year HispanicBusiness.com lists the Top 25 Hispanic nonprofits and, for 2011, the list included organizations whose annual revenues range from $10.5 million to $182 million. With missions that focus on the empowerment of neighborhoods, preventative health-care services and access to post-secondary educational opportunities, these charities have stayed true to supporting the vital needs of their communities (W. K. Kellogg Foundation, 2012). Latino philanthropists are supporting these organizations in great numbers and much of the choice regarding which philanthropic organizations to support is based on the concept of *pluralismo*. *Pluralismo* refers to the decision process involved in giving – the more knowledge about the organization or the recipient, the more likely the gift (Duran, 2001).

PHILOSOPHY OF LATINO PHILANTHROPY

Latino philanthropy dates back to the 1500s, but has rarely been documented (Miranda, 1999). It began through a system of informal charities. Many Latinos believe that giving will bring them closer to God as much of Latino giving is based on the individual's relationship with the church – "When you give to the Lord, the Lord will always be faithful to you" (Royce & Rodriguez, 1999, p. 16). Latino culture is deeply tied to the church, and in many cases, it is the Catholic Church. Seventy percent of Latinos in the United States identify as Catholic. In fact, the Catholic Church receives the majority of Latino philanthropy (Hall-Russell & Kasberg, 1997; Wagner & Hall-Russell, 1999).

When we first began conducting research for this book, we thought that mainly new immigrants would hold this commitment to the Catholic Church as a way of maintaining a connection with their home country. However, we found this faith tradition to be followed just as closely by the younger generation of Latinos, including those that are second and third generation Americans (W. K. Kellogg Foundation, 2012). For example, just recently, one of us was a part of a philanthropy-focused committee that included several individuals representing different Latino cultures. With many organizations, during the initial meeting, members were asked to share information about themselves and their reasons for joining the group. One Latina, when asked about her reasons for joining, said: "For as far back as I can remember, my grandmother constantly reminded me and my cousins that the only sure way of getting into heaven was to give to the church. I believed it then and to this day, I preach the very same message to my children." When asked if she was a first generation American, she said "No, actually I'm third generation."

Of note, some Latinos, depending on country of origin, need to be educated about formal philanthropy (Ramos, 1999). In many South American countries as well as Mexico, the services provided by nonprofits are often covered by the government, making it unnecessary to have the philanthropic network that we have in the United States. The government and churches provide the majority of community services such as youth, senior citizens' programs and health care and that expectation is placed on these American entities when new immigrants move to the United States (Osili & Du, 2005; Ramos, 1999). As such, the U.S. form of philanthropy, where nonprofits mitigate social inequalities, is still an emerging concept. Of course, this lack of understanding applies more to first-time, unseasoned donors as well as to newer immigrants. More assimilated donors have a greater understanding of the United States' complex "system" of government and philanthropic programs working hand in hand (W. K. Kellogg Foundation, 2012).

Much like African American giving, Latino giving often does not register using traditional measures of philanthropy such as those produced by Giving USA or Independent Sector (Marx & Carter, 2008). Year after year, these mainstream, formal surveys have failed to understand the essence of Latino philanthropy. These surveys claim that Latinos give a lower percentage of their income to charity. However, other surveys that control for income, education, and immigrant status show that Latinos give at the same rate or higher than the majority of the population (Cortés, 2002; Osili & Du, 2005). In addition, according to a survey by Direct Marking News conducted in 1993, Latino households are rarely solicited as compared to other racial and ethnic groups, receiving 15 direct mail pieces per year on average, compared to the 300 that other minorities receive. As we all know, not being asked is the number one reason why people do not give (Ramos & Kasper, 2000).

Giving in Latino culture is often in-kind and to family and friends, much like that of other racial and ethnic groups (Ramos & Kasper, 2000). Low-income and even middle-class Latinos give often and in increasing amounts, particularly to emergency events such as hurricanes or earthquakes in Latin America as well as community needs (Duran, 2001; Ford Foundation, 2003; W. K. Kellogg Foundation, 2012). According to Marcelina Rivera, the former executive director of the Latino Community Foundation of Colorado, "While Latinos have traditionally been givers, we have done so quietly, often through family and religious institutions. Now we're asking people to stand up and be counted by doing their giving in a public, strategic, and collective way" (Duran, 2001, p. 37).

Among Latinos, there are vast differences in terms of class and generational status. Those Latinos that have been in the United States longer are much more likely to give to organized philanthropy and mainstream nonprofits. However, new immigrants often are unaware of the organizations or lack trust (Osili & Du, 2005). According to Ramos (1999), "a significant number of the wealthy and influential Latinos . . . say that they are equally likely to give to both mainstream and Latino organizations" (p. 160). Moreover, these more affluent Latinos give substantial amounts of their time and money to organizations such as the March of Dimes and the American Heart Association. They also give to major colleges and universities throughout the nation. Research shows that mainstream giving is on the rise among middle-class donors as well, demonstrating that Latinos and Whites donate at the same rate to the United Way (W. K. Kellogg Foundation, 2012). According to Ramos (1999), over time Latino giving begins to mirror mainstream giving.

In order to learn more about philanthropy and being philanthropic, Latinos need to be included on nonprofit and foundation boards. In 1999, Latinos constituted only 0.5 percent of foundations and other boards of directors and trustees (Sanchez & Zamora, 1999). Fast-forward 13 years, Latinos now represent 3.5 percent of nonprofit board membership (*Nonprofit Quarterly*, May 2012). While a significant increase, these percentages are nowhere near representative of Latinos in the population. The lack of growth in this area is consistent with the limited funding foundations provide to Latino causes. Often referred to as the "invisible minority" these forms of omission by foundations probably contribute to the virtual non-existence of engagement of Latinos in traditional philanthropy (Cortés, 1999).

In researching the giving habits of younger, more upwardly mobile Hispanics, one of the constant themes we heard was that there was an absence of people who resemble them in leadership roles. For example, one Latino said, "While I am grateful for traditional nonprofits helping to uplift our culture, the time has come for us now to be included in decision making. Each time I am solicited by a national organization, I immediately go to their website and look for diversity on the board. If there is none, which is often the case, I generally will not give" (Armando Rayo, personal communication, March, 2011). Continued failure on the part of mainstream foundations and nonprofits to include Latino representation has certainly contributed to the deficiency in the culture's participation rate.

GIVING PATTERNS BY LATINO ETHNIC GROUPS

There is great variation among the various Latino cultures. As such, we have provided a brief overview of some sub-ethnic groups.

Mexicans

According to Duran (2001), "Since the U.S.-Mexican War ended in 1848, there has been a flow of Mexican immigrants to the southwestern United States, who joined long-established Mexican-American communities in Texas, New Mexico, Colorado, Arizona, and California" (p. 43). And these communities created *mutualista* (mutual aid) organizations, which were designed to assist new immigrants as they settled in the United States. *Mutualistas* also provide burial plans and served as a community insurance pool. Moreover, they assisted local community members in the fight against racism, which immigrants encountered on a regular basis (Duran, 2001). *Mutualistas* served social networks, often sponsoring celebrations (fiestas) and dances. They supported low-income members of the Mexican population, including fighting for the right to vote, better schools and services for Mexican American communities (Duran, 2001). Unfortunately, these *Mutualistas* have been left out of traditional discussions of philanthropy.

Although all Latino groups send remittances to relatives in their country of origin, Mexicans send the largest amount, roughly $4 billion a year, providing Mexico's second largest source of foreign income after oil (Duran, 2001; Multilateral Investment Fund Inter-American Development Bank, 2003; Pettey, 2002). And, after tourism and oil, remittances are the third largest source of income in Mexico. These remittances support church renovations, roads, family needs, and even the digging of village wells (Duran, 2001; Multilateral Investment Fund Inter-American Development Bank, 2003; Pettey, 2002).

Puerto Ricans

Puerto Ricans are substantially different from Mexican immigrants because they are part of the United States. However, because Puerto Rico is physically separate from the continental United States, it has unique traditions and those individuals who move to the mainland also have unique perspectives that they bring with them. Puerto Rican philanthropists often use giving and volunteering as a way to gain credibility and access to more mainstream leaders and organizations. This strategy aims to enlighten majority America to the issues and needs that are important to Latinos. In addition, increased exposure, especially through volunteerism, helps to quell misconceptions and insensitivities toward Puerto Ricans and Latinos in general (Ramos, 1999).

Puerto Ricans have used nonprofit organizations and associations as a primary method of assimilating into mainstream American culture. Since the 1800s, the Puerto Rican community has used a system of mutual aid societies to support their people, especially in New York City. New York has the largest group of Puerto Rican nonprofits, fostering giving among this community and serving the needs of young and old (Ford Foundation, 2003).

Of note, Puerto Ricans, as well as some other Latinos, even when middle class, are not interested in supporting endowments. Latinos are interested in giving to organizations that tackle immediate needs and do not think that endowments are the best use of funds. Of course, greater education as to the importance of endowment giving might engender more giving in this area. Providing alternative methods for giving is vital to increasing Latino philanthropy (Ramos, 1999).

Cubans

Cuban Americans are often viewed distinctly from other Latinos because they tend to be more politically conservative. They are also often better educated and more affluent (Ford Foundation, 2003; W. K. Kellogg Foundation, 2012). Researchers see the Cuban approach to philanthropy as being different than other Latinos. For example, there is some argument over whether or not Cubans send remittances like other Latino immigrants with some researchers claiming that Cubans adhere to the economic embargo against Cuba (Ford Foundation, 2003; Multilateral Investment Fund Inter-American Development Bank, 2003; Pettey, 2002). Among Cuban Americans, philanthropy is often used as an "important bridge to the mainstream" (Ramos, 1999,

p. 163). To Cuban donors, it is essential that they be seen as givers to society rather than as mere takers. They want to be seen as contributors to the greater good in American society and consider giving to the larger world an obligation. Cuban Americans are most likely to develop foundations, be they family foundations or Latino community foundations, to foster giving (Holley, 2003). They see foundations as a way to increase ownership and use that ownership as a way to develop more community-controlled philanthropy. Cuban donors are similar to other Latinos in that they give to the church and family first, but they are interested in acculturation opportunities and are deeply inclined to fund causes that support self-sustaining activities and self-sufficiency. They want to work hand in hand with the mainstream community but also want to be viewed as a group of immigrants and former immigrants that takes care of itself (Osili & Du, 2005). They are particularly interested in philanthropic opportunities that are responsive to Latino issues and that speak to current civil rights issues for this community.

Latin Americans

Smith et al. (1999) found that Latin Americans, especially newer immigrants, give little time and money to mainstream non-profits, with the exception of churches. Instead, they give to family and communities outside the United States with which they feel close. Smith et al. (1999) determined from their research that Latin Americans were distrustful of more formal philanthropy and organizations as these types of organizations, outside of the church, were not prominent in their homelands. According to Cortés (2002), Latin American giving goes to the family first but the very definition of family is much more expansive than traditional definitions of the nuclear family in the United States. For example, among Guatemalans and Salvadoreans, giving food and providing shelter to new

American immigrants was a traditional way of being philanthropic. Guatemalans, in particular, did not give to mainstream philanthropy because they felt that it was ignorant of
Guatemalan and other Latin American cultures to do so. They
also found it to be impersonal and greedy in its approach. On the
other hand, Salvadoreans were much more willing and likely to
give to well-established nonprofits, although they still found
these organizations to be untrustworthy. Miranda (1999) has
speculated about the reasons for the lack of trust and attributes
it to violations of the civil rights of Latinos in the United States.
He notes that many Latin Americans have created their own
foundations as a way of defending their communities against
"public and private prejudice and bias" (p. 53).

MOTIVATIONS FOR LATINO GIVING

There is a common phrase shared among various Latino groups,
"*la importancia de la palaabra*" (the importance of one's word),
which speaks to their belief in the value and importance of
personal relationships. Latinos traditionally prefer hands-on
solicitation and cultivation from someone within their community and who is highly respected (Ramos, 1999). In many
cases, the person making "the ask" is equally or, in some
instances, more important than the charitable cause for which
the solicitation is being made. With this in mind, face-to-face
interactions, especially with first and second generation Latinos,
will always prove to be more effective than direct mail
approaches.

This is not to say that college fundraisers will need to meet
with all Hispanic alumni, but identifying a few potential donors
that are established or up-and-coming in communities where
there is a significant alumni presence, is certainly a starting
point. From there, fundraisers should arrange a meeting with
these individuals to share the college or university's goal of

engaging more alumni of color and request their assistance in galvanizing the efforts of others in the area. This could lead to a greater level of participation.

WHERE LATINOS GIVE AND WHY

There are many reasons why Latinos give and some of these are similar to other ethnic and racial minorities. First and foremost, Latinos provide funds for emergency assistance. Because hurricanes and earthquakes often hit their homelands, they reach out to those in need in their home countries (W. K. Kellogg Foundation, 2012). Among those Latinos that immigrated to the United States there is a sense of obligation. Those already in the country help others become acclimated to a new place and assist with food, shelter, employment, and clothing (Duran, 2001).

Latinos also give in the area of education (Marx & Carter, 2008; Parra, 1999; Rodriguez, 1999). Whereas there has always existed a more deliberate spotlight on giving to education among donors of color, Latinos and their success or lack of success in school makes education a formidable reason to focus on it. Consider the following: Latinos now account for nearly one in four school-age children in the United States (Royce & Rodriguez, 1999). However, in the coming decades, Latinos will make up one-third to one half of students in school systems across the nation. Only about half of Latinos entering their freshman year will graduate high school in four years; less than 10 percent of Latinos have a college degree; one in 20 public high school teachers in science or math is Latino. Education is a ripe area in terms of giving among Latinos. There is an allegiance to the education system in the United States for uplifting several generations of Latinos while at the same time there is a commitment among Latinos to support those who are struggling to earn an education (Rodriguez, 1999).

There is also great promise in terms of philanthropic investment at the higher education level. Long-term investment in Latino education is needed. In fact, academically qualified Latino students are often disrupted on the road to college by the low expectations of teachers, lack of knowledge of the college admissions and financial aid processes, and little parental support. Other barriers include linguistic access, limited entry for undocumented students, and poverty. Of Latinos who cut their education short during or right after high school, three out of four say they did so because they had to support their family. All of these issues are significant and beg for more support among Latino (and other) donors. They are areas around which to engage potential donors (Rodriguez, 1999).

Research has found that Latinos support programs that address the barriers to Latino educational attainment by engaging entire families in educational decisions, providing funding, and making education more affordable (W. K. Kellogg Foundation, 2012). They also support community-driven initiatives that promote Latino success in education, specifically around issues of curriculum, language, effective teachers, and treatment of immigrants. According to researchers, the Latino focus on education is consistent with other donors of color. To most minorities, education is seen as a tool for both individual and collective forms of empowerment (Rodriguez, 1999).

Within the realm of educational philanthropy, Latinos give about a third of their support to scholarships. According to Duran (2001), "Although scholarship funding has not traditionally been seen as a social change strategy among mainstream philanthropy, in the context of identity-based funds it has significant symbolic value because it speaks to core values around fairness and access while addressing real and immediate disparities" (p. 17). Moreover, scholarships can transform lives and those who have benefited from them in the past want to give to the next generation.

A fair amount of Latino philanthropy goes to the poor. Poverty is an important issue to many Latinos as so many immigrants hailed from struggling countries and also struggled financially when they came to the United States. Once people become successful they are often eager to help others, even in small ways. Much of this philanthropy is directed to the basic needs, food, and shelter of the less fortunate (W. K. Kellogg Foundation, 2001, 2012).

Latinos give to arts and culture at a greater rate than other racial and ethnic minorities (Ford Foundation, 2003). They are especially inclined to support cultural and art organizations that celebrate and highlight Latino art forms and Latino traditions for broader audiences. According to Ramos (1999), Latino donors support these artistic endeavors for two main reasons. First, "they enjoy and take great pride in Latino Culture and want it to be more accessible within their own communities" (p. 165), and second, "they believe that exposing a broader audience to Latino arts is an important strategic investment in expanded mainstream appreciation of Latino culture and societal contribution" (p. 165). Latino culture is deeply rooted in the arts and there is a tremendous amount of cultural pride (Ramos, 1999).

Much like Asian Americans, Latinos invest in their elders. Often these individuals live with their children. Latinos support health, social, and recreational services for their relatives as well as for the elderly members of their communities. Although Latinos are a relatively young population, there are three million Latinos that are 65 years or older living in the United States, and this population is growing at a considerable rate. According to Duran (2001), a "Latino age wave" is on its way and by the year 2050, older Latinos will make up 13 percent of all U.S. citizens (p. 37). This figure is nearly as big as the proportion of all Latinos today. More specifically, between 2008 and 2030 the Latino population aged 65 years and older will increase by 224 percent compared to a 65 percent increase for the White population aged 65 and older (U.S. Census, 2010).

This elderly Latino population faces significant challenges. According to a report by the Pew Hispanic Center (2010), older Latinos are twice as likely to be poor than the general population. These older immigrants are more likely to need social security to support their daily needs but often do not qualify for these benefits. In addition, older Latinos often face diabetes and other deadly diseases. Unfortunately, language, economic, and cultural barriers often prevent older Latinos from receiving proper health care. Researchers estimate that the federal government is not prepared to support the older Latino population (Pew Hispanic Center, 2010). However, there are many community-based nonprofit organizations that do provide the necessary services to the Latino elderly. They are being supported, for the most part, by other Latinos, but will need additional resources to meet the needs of the older Latino population.

Another area of interest for Latino donors is youth programs and services (W. K. Kellogg Foundation, 2012). Currently, more than six million Latino children live in poverty. This figure is greater than the child poverty rate for any other racial and ethnic group. Currently one in four school-age children is Latino, with more than half of these children being male. Latino males, in particular, have many pressing needs. For example, their homicide rate is five times higher than that of White males. Latino male children and young adults are less likely to have health insurance. Compounding the lack of health insurance is the fact that Latino boys face the greatest health risks, especially in terms of HIV/AIDs. There are several Latino-led organizations that are addressing these important issues. They are the kind of organizations that Latino donors support in that they are culturally rooted and relevant (Duran, 2001).

As mentioned, the Catholic Church is a major recipient of Latino philanthropy and a significant shaper of Latino giving patterns (Duran, 2001). Most religious giving among Latinos was once exclusively to the Catholic Church, but in more recent years, fundamentalist Christian churches have reached out in great numbers, lessening the overall amount of money the Catholic Church receives. Of note, many Latino cultural events are tied to the Church and also involve opportunities for giving to the Church directly – either to family members, community members, or in honor of someone (Ramos, 1999).

Another commonality with Asian American and Pacific Islanders that Latinos have is an interest in supporting human rights causes. In the case of Latinos, immigration is one of the most salient human rights issues and there is growing support for programs related to advocacy as well as services for immigrants. There is also Latino donor support for English as a Second Language (ESL) and citizenship classes, legal services, and adult education classes. These are all significant needs for Latino immigrants, especially those wanting to enter the U.S. workforce (Duran, 2011).

The last major area of philanthropic giving for Latinos is remittance (Multilateral Investment Fund Inter-American Development Bank, 2003; Pettey, 2002). We mentioned this earlier but as it is highly significant, we want to dedicate more time to the topic. According to Duran (2001), Latino immigrants send more than 10 percent of their annual income back to their families and hometowns. Currently, $25 billion in remittance is sent to Latin and South American countries. It is estimated that 70 percent of Latino immigrants send remittance on a regular basis (Multilateral Investment Fund Inter-American Development Bank, 2003; Pettey, 2003).

BEST APPROACHES TO ENGAGING AND SOLICITING LATINO ALUMNI

Latinos enjoy seeing their giving at work, meaning they want to see tangible, measurable, and quantifiable results. As a development officer, having someone on the fundraising team create a list of campus cultural events, past and present, that showcases accomplishments can be an initial way of generating interest in the institution. This type of information can be shared with older alumni who may have attended the university at a time when these activities were not as plentiful. Another potential constituent group that would most likely appreciate learning of such efforts is the Latino community outside of the university. In many instances, schools may be recognized nationally as one of the highly touted institutions in the nation due to their success in sports and academics; however, to those in the neighboring community, there may be no connection or involvement of any kind.

At the University of North Carolina, Chapel Hill, for example, the Carolina Latina/o Collaborative produces an annual report highlighting the joint effort of university officials, faculty, staff, students, and community members to empower Latinos. This engagement, which serves as a collaborative process to explore how Carolina may become more inclusive of Latina/o communities and cultures, is a top-down driven initiative as the Office for Diversity and Multicultural Affairs, and Student Affairs, are each heavily involved in the implementation.

Recently, the Collaboration expanded its reach to an even broader audience as they hosted a White House Hispanic Community Action Summit to accomplish three goals:

1. Establish a space where community leaders can meaningfully engage and interact with key decision and policy makers in the Obama Administration on matters involving diverse policy areas that affect the Hispanic community.

2. Identify policy and programmatic areas of concern, receive and respond to constructive criticism and feedback, and identify local success stories and practices in policy areas that benefit the Hispanic community and our nation.

3. Identify and develop opportunities for Hispanic leaders and stakeholders to collaborate with the Obama Administration and other leaders from across the country in addressing the interests and concerns of the Hispanic community.

This initiative is visible and attractive to potential Latino donors.

Another quantifiable way of giving is scholarships. Latinos are greatly concerned with education and their access to it. How many Latino students received scholarships at your institution this past year? The last five years? Are scholarships being used to attract Latino students? What are the retention and graduation rates of Latino students over the last decade? Presenting questions such as these and their corresponding answers to Latino church or community leaders could potentially sway attention and engagement toward the institution.

Latinos are concerned with social and human rights issues as are all alumni of color. At this point in time, most Americans have heard of the Arizona Immigration Law that:

- Makes it a crime under state law to be in the country illegally by specifically requiring immigrants to have proof of their immigration status.
- Requires police officers to "make a reasonable attempt" to determine the immigration status of a person if there is a "reasonable suspicion" that he or she is an illegal immigrant.

Whether your institution is for or against this law, a large percentage of Latinos are against it, which includes some college and university alumni. Hosting speakers or debates on campus to discuss this issue and others like it is a good way to engage Latino alumni. Social justice causes are vitally important to Latinos. This is most likely due to the long history of discrimination against Spanish-speaking immigrants (Duran, 2001).

One of the major issues impeding the success of Latino giving is that Latinos are rarely asked to be trustees of philanthropic organizations, limiting their engagement and their enthusiasm about giving. Too often only a few Latino leaders are asked over and over to serve while the majority of the community is ignored. Expanding the pool of Latinos on boards could lead to greater giving and greater partnerships between Latino communities and mainstream philanthropy.

Like the AAPI community, Latino culture is deeply diverse. Development and alumni staff members need to understand this diversity and respect it. In addition, they must pay attention to the Latino community's deep commitment to church, family, and culture. Engaging Latinos seriously around these issues will lead to greater giving, both in-kind and financially.

5

NATIVE AMERICAN PHILANTHROPY AND ALUMNI

"Community over Individual"

Although Native Americans constitute one of the most impoverished segments of the United States, they have made great strides in the past two decades through entrepreneurial and commercial activities that draw on tribal strengths and sovereign status. Consumer spending research indicates that, in 2010, Native Americans contributed over $12 billion to the American economy. And in some states, such as Wisconsin, Minnesota, Arizona, and New Mexico, Native Americans contributed nearly 20 percent of the state's income. Native American-owned businesses are also becoming major forces in terms of employment in states such as Minnesota and New Mexico (Berry, 1999). According to the U.S. Census Bureau, over the past 20 years, Native American businesses have increased by nearly 100 percent.

Although there is great poverty in Native American communities, these individuals should not be looked upon as the recipients of philanthropy and services only. They are a philanthropic people and to think otherwise reinforces stereotypes (Berry, 1999). According to Berry (1999), the new wealth in Native American communities, "combined with an innate generosity, offers the larger philanthropic community a unique opportunity to reach out to those who once were on the fringe of social, political and economic systems, and enable them to participate more fully and equally in civic and community affairs" (p. 35). More importantly, Berry notes that a new strategy would "alter perspectives of Native Americans from dependent and poor to creative and generous" (p. 35).

Native Americans make up less than 1 percent of the student population of colleges and universities across the country (National Center for Education Statistics, 2010). Yet, at many institutions in the West and Southwest, they make up significant percentages. And, their representation is growing at some Southern and Southeastern colleges. In addition, Native Americans attend the nation's 32 tribal colleges and universities.

Often when we present at national conferences on Native American philanthropy, people ask whether it is even necessary to include this group as it does not constitute a large enough percentage of the potential alumni population to garner an investment of time and money. However, to not include Native Americans is to ignore a significant group of people in the nation. Moreover, Native American culture is deeply rooted in giving and there is much to learn from its approach.

The larger Native American community is quite diverse. Each tribal community has its own customs and traditions (Edmunds, 1995). Philanthropy has always been practiced, with various forms of giving centered on spirituality, art, and family (W. K. Kellogg Foundation, 2012). As mentioned, some tribal communities have had economic success in recent years – such as the Seminoles in Florida – and as such their philanthropy has become more formal and even institutionalized. In cases in which the tribes have substantial income, their giving is typically focused on organizations that serve the most members of their tribe (Nielsen, Hovila, & Nielsen, 2010). According to Berry (1999), Native Americans are modeling some of their strategies on mainstream philanthropy. For example, they are forming partnerships with other Native as well as non-Native organizations as a way of "achieving self-sufficiency and self-determination as well as leveraging human and financial resources" (p. 31). They are also establishing tribal foundations and incorporating them under tribal law (Nielsen et al., 2010). This approach enables them to "protect their sovereignty and independence and contribute to tribal services and infrastructure needs" (p. 31). Berry (1999) also claims that some tribal communities are beginning to develop tribal community foundations as a way for the tribal members to assist with "quality of life enhancements" such as health, housing, and the environment (p. 31).

Although limited, Native Americans have created several organizations aimed at fostering philanthropic giving on a larger scale, with a goal of enhancing Native American independence and building stronger self-identities. Native Americans have started organizations such as the First Nations Development Institute, the Seventh Generation Fund for Indian Development, and the American Indian College Fund (W. K. Kellogg Foundation, 2012). The Hopi Foundation, for example, boasts a mission "to promote self-sufficiency, self-reliance, and local self-determination among the Hopi people" (W. K. Kellogg Foundation, 2012, p. 67). It is one of the very first independent Native American foundations and

> provides grants, technical assistance, and other services to villages and nonprofit organizations serving the Hopi people. Its services and programs address a range of social and economic issues on the reservation – including unemployment, poverty, and violence – while

also promoting the preservation and celebration of traditional values and customs.

W. K. Kellogg Foundation, 2012, p. 67

The Hopi Foundation, as well as the others mentioned, encourage large-scale giving and invest in areas such as education and economic empowerment (Nielsen et al., 2010).

PHILOSOPHY OF NATIVE AMERICAN PHILANTHROPY

Within Native cultures, giving and receiving is considered honorable (Edmunds, 1995). The practice is revered. Moreover, giving is circular and is constantly in motion. It moves from one person to the next with the underlying notion that if you are given to, you will give to others. In the words of Duran (2001) "In traditional Native-American societies, giving is a form of sharing, not charity, that bonds you within the group, because you have provided a series of gifts that allow the group to prosper" (p. 68). Unlike mainstream philanthropy, which often links giving to power and prestige, Native American giving is an "extension of honor to the generations to come and to other kin or clan members. Giving symbolizes an expression of interest in the larger world" (Berry, 1999, p. 44). Moreover, whereas mainstream philanthropy is linked to wealth based on inherited monies and property, Native American philanthropy is based on the idea of sharing resources and knowledge to uplift (W. K. Kellogg Foundation, 2001, 2012). Mainstream philanthropy is based on an uneven power dynamic, with the giver offering a gift to the receiver, who must be grateful in the acceptance. The gift is not mutual. In Native communities, gifts are spiritual in nature and based on mutual respect (Berry, 1999). Native American philanthropy is also tied to preserving the future generation of Native people. Philanthropy that uplifts the surrounding community and complements it is encouraged.

One of the most important aspects of Native American philanthropy is the notion that the community is more important than the individual (Edmunds, 1995). This is fundamentally different to mainstream philanthropy or overarching ideas in the United States. We are a nation built on the idea of individual success and achieving the American dream. This idea is antithetical to Native culture as Native Americans are more focused on uplifting the entire community. Bringing attention to oneself as an individual is not a natural part of Native culture. The mainstream worldview focuses on personal property rights and wealth accumulation whereas Native communities believe in communal ownership and the redistribution of wealth. For example, according to LaDonna Harris, who holds membership in the Comanche Indian Tribe, "you should never own anything that can't be given away" (Berry, 1999, p. 45). Although mainstream philanthropists can be wonderfully altruistic, the notion put forth by Harris seems to buck up against the very foundation of mainstream society, which emphasizes possessions and accumulation. These vast differences in worldviews result in unique understandings of philanthropy (Berry, 1999).

The support of immediate and extended family are also important within the realm of philanthropy. Native Americans participate in informal giving and do so through potlatches, or gift-giving ceremonies, and activities that reflect the "regional and local characteristics" of the tribes (Duran, 2001, p. 69). Much of this kind of giving is reflective of early giving between European settlers and Native tribes – it is based on a system of needs and exchanges. Moreover, potlatches offer Native Americans an opportunity to give away wealth to those close to them and in need (W. K. Kellogg Foundation, 2012). Giving away wealth is a deeply rooted notion in most Native communities. In addition, Native American family structure includes extended families and encourages working together across extended families. Giving among families emphasizes reciprocity. According to Delgado

(2003), it is advantageous to tap into these networks when working with Native American donors.

Native American philanthropy is shaped by language, religion, and cultural practices and, historically, much of the giving within Native communities has been focused on bringing elders, community leaders, youth, and medicine people together to meet the goals of individual Native communities (Delgado, 2003). Native people focus on growing the community and promoting a healthy environment. There is also an emphasis on finding solutions to problems that plague Native Americans communities as well as Native individuals.

Some philanthropic support has come in the form of political support for sovereignty. There is a fear among some tribal leaders that Indian nation sovereignty will be taken away by the federal government because Native Americans make up such a small percentage of the population.

MOTIVATIONS FOR NATIVE AMERICAN GIVING

Researchers have identified a variety of motivations for giving among Native Americans. First, Native people are interested in distributing wealth throughout and among Native communities. They want to see parity and, by giving, this parity can be achieved. Second, Native Americans want to address community needs and are willing to invest funds in order to reshape their communities. They have a communal obligation. For example, some Native people pledge their service to their tribe and their community, committing to volunteerism as well as giving money to the larger community (Berry, 1999). Third, there is a great interest in empowering tribal communities for positive change and to enhance their political power. Providing philanthropic support for these efforts is essential in that mainstream foundations give less than 1 percent of their funding to Native American causes, and unfortunately most of that funding is given to non-

Indian controlled organizations that profess to serve Native Americans (Delgado, 2003). Within Native communities, there is a strong feeling that non-Native organizations are not interested in positive change and instead are operating with their own agenda and motives. According to Delgado (2003), "Native nonprofits are more likely than all nonprofits in the U.S. to be involved in economic and community development, probably due to the socioeconomic discrepancies between Native Americans and the U.S. population as a whole" (p. 12). It should be noted that Native Americans are willing to engage with mainstream philanthropic organizations but these institutions have to demonstrate that they have diversity on their boards and staff before there will be great engagement and giving.

CHARACTERISTICS OF NATIVE AMERICAN DONORS

There are two main characteristics of Native American donors. First, they are insular in that Native American donors are the least likely of all racial and ethnic groups to step out of their comfort zone and give to non-Native causes and communities. Second, unlike Asian Americans and Pacific Islanders, prestige or rank does not matter to Native Americans in terms of giving. They are not motivated to give by influential individuals, but rather causes related to building up the Native community. The Native American aversion to prestige is linked to differences in decision-making and relationships. For example, in Native cultures decisions are made using consensus and when positive results take place from the decisions, the entire group is credited. This is vastly different from the mainstream United States, which places emphasis on hierarchal decision making and also attributes successes to the leaders of a group or organization rather than the group members as a whole (Berry, 1999).

WHERE NATIVE AMERICANS GIVE AND WHY

First and foremost, Native Americans give to those who are close to them. As noted above, they are motivated to give by family issues and relationships. Of course, this type of philanthropy does not register with national organizations that capture giving but it is philanthropy nonetheless. As with other donors, Native Americans prefer to have a close familiarity with the group or individual asking them to give. Of note and great importance, many Native people prefer to give anonymously (Duran, 2001; Nielsen et al., 2010). They see giving as representing reciprocity and a gift to "the Creator and to the community" rather than prestige or altruism (Berry, 1999, p. 54). Moreover, modesty is a major tenet of Native American cultures and publicity related to personal wealth or personal accomplishments runs counter to the fundamental beliefs of tribal communities (Berry, 1999). In fact, according to a United Way survey, completed in 1999, the majority of Native American donors prefer to know what happens to their donations, but they are not interested in being publically recognized for their generosity (Berry, 1999).

Second, Native Americans donate to tribal charities. According to Duran (2001), research shows that the Native American tribes that are "more traditional tend to consider the cultural and spiritual relevance of their giving more important than do more progressive tribes. The latter consider education, the arts, economic development, and entertainment as important causes for which to give" (p. 69). Research also shows that those donors based on a reservation demonstrate differences in giving when compared to those Native Americans who do not or have not lived on a reservation. Those who live on the reservation tend to support tribal charities, individual members of their tribe, recreational activities, and educational activities (Duran, 2001). Those Native Americans that are not on reservations tend to support more mainstream historical and cultural projects as well as social services and church activities (Duran, 2001; W. K. Kellogg Foundation, 2012). Another factor that makes a difference in where Native Americans give is where their wealth is derived. If wealth comes from their individual work, Native Americans are more likely to donate to mainstream causes, but if the wealth is acquired through their tribe or tribal activities, they are unlikely to be adventurous in their giving.

Third, Native Americans give to educational programs. The Native American population in general is severely under-educated and as such much of Native philanthropy is directed toward educational issues. For example, according to Delgado (2003), much philanthropy goes to immersion schools, which "are a proven vehicle for transmitting culture and language, and they improve performance in other areas as well" (p. 21). In addition, Native Americans support tribal colleges, which play an important role in Native communities, providing meeting places, libraries, and adult education (Delgado, 2003; Gasman, Baez, and Turner, 2007). There is also an interest in giving to programs that reduce the high school dropout rate and those that focus on preparing Native American teachers. Education is a likely outlet for Native American giving because giving to educational causes is concrete and tangible. One can easily see results. The majority of Native donors want to see results from their donation before they give again.

Fourth, Native Americans care about cultural preservation as well as economic growth. They are willing to invest in and support efforts to create more accurate portrayals of Native Americans, often supporting efforts that present truthful histories and the current realities of Native people (Delgado, 2003). There has been an increase in Native American foundations and they are focused on preserving culture and expanding knowledge.

Fifth, there is a strong focus on taking care of the community elders. Much like Latinos and Asian American and Pacific

Islander donors, Native Americans give to causes that support services for the elderly as well as health-related programs focused on improving the lives of the elderly.

Sixth, Native donors give substantially to both tribe-related programs focused on drugs and alcohol as well as more mainstream services aimed at assisting with drug and alcohol addiction. Drug and alcohol addiction is a substantial problem in Native communities. Both of these substances are sought out to quell depression, which is a significant concern, especially on reservations. Native donors give to both practical programs as well as research-focused programs related to these issues. Related to drug and alcohol addiction is the issue of poverty. Much Native philanthropy is directed toward bettering the lives of other Native Americans who suffer in poverty.

One of the most important aspects of Native American philanthropy is respect for culture. Those mainstream organizations and fundraisers looking to work with Native American donors must keep in mind that most giving is done at the local level, needs to be respectful of traditions, and should honor diverse ways of giving (Berry, 1999).

BEST APPROACHES TO ENGAGING AND SOLICITING NATIVE AMERICAN ALUMNI

Native Americans are the most unique in terms of philanthropy and as potential donors. Because Native communities are somewhat insular, development officers must use very different strategies when engaging and soliciting them for involvement in the campus community. First and foremost, all outreach must convey a sense of respect and honor for Indian cultural traditions and individual dignity (Berry, 1999; Nielsen et al., 2010). If working directly with tribal communities rather than individuals, it is important to engage the elders of these communities. Second, those engaging Native donors should build on existing relationships within communities and encourage giving circles (Nielsen et al., 2010). Community leaders can be engaged to speak about giving within tribal communities and within mainstream communities. However, these leaders need to be listened to and engaged in realistic and meaningful ways. Too often organizations want a token Native American member of their boards and alumni association leadership, but they do not want to listen to alternative voices (Nielsen et al., 2010). Third, links need to be made in order to empower Native communities so that they are not dependent on mainstream cultures. Lastly, fundraising solicitations should be linked to fighting injustice and meeting the needs of Native people.

Those in alumni and development offices on college and university campuses know very little about Native American cultures and often neglect to engage these groups due to their small numbers. However, Native American traditions shed light on new ways of thinking about philanthropy and can influence approaches to engagement with all alumni. Furthermore, engaging Native American alumni serves as motivation for increased involvement among Native American individuals and Native communities on college campuses.

6

A CONVERSATION WITH ADVANCEMENT STAFF AT MAJORITY INSTITUTIONS

In trying to understand outreach and engagement of alumni of color at majority institutions, we surveyed and interviewed those institutions with membership in the American Association of Universities (AAU) (see appendices). The AAU focuses on issues that are important to "research-intensive universities, such as funding for research, research policy issues, and graduate and undergraduate education." Moreover, AAU member institutions are on "the leading edge of innovation, scholarship, and solutions that contribute to the nation's economy, security, and well-being" (AAU website, 2012). We chose these institutions because they are representative of the types of institutions that have, in most cases, made recent efforts to reach out to students of color in order to diversify their student bodies. In this chapter, we highlight the results of both the survey and interviews, examining the landscape of American higher education in terms of commitment to alumni of color and highlighting some of the best practices being used at institutions throughout the country.

According to our survey results, 100 percent of the respondents had some kind of association(s) for alumni of color or some type of network for engaging and communicating with this group of alumni. By and large, the majority of efforts are directed toward Black and Latino alumni, with very little emphasis on Native Americans and Asian Americans and Pacific Islanders (with the exception of the Californian institutions). One of the main ways that these institutions engage alumni of color is through reunions, with 70 percent of the institutions hosting events that are specifically for alumni of color. Some institutions separate alumni of color by racial and ethnic group while others lump all alumni of color together. Unlike their White counterparts, alumni of color do not attend alumni weekends at the same rate. Of those institutions surveyed for this book, 90 percent said that alumni of color participate at a lower rate. Given research related to the engagement of alumni of color (or the lack thereof) this response makes sense. Alumni of color are less likely to engage because they are not asked in ways that are relevant to their lives and interests. However, there is much potential here as noted in the 2012 W. K. Kellogg Foundation report *Cultures of Giving*. This report details the changing landscape of philanthropy and generosity of people of color.

One of the main issues in terms of resistance to engaging alumni of color is a belief that it is not worth it and that there will not be a return on the investment. However, this notion is based on little evidence. According to our survey respondents, 60 percent track giving levels among alumni of color, but most have only been doing so for the past five years. Of those who do track giving amongst alumni of color, 30 percent noted that these alumni contribute 5 percent of all annual giving. The remaining 10 percent of our respondents stated that alumni of color contribute 10 percent of all annual giving. It is important to note that of the group of institutions tracking data, the overall alumni of color population is roughly 15 percent so these contribution levels are relatively high.

As the population of students of color grows on campuses across the country so does the future alumni. We were curious as to how our survey participants were dealing with the future influx of alumni of color and asked if the institutions had specific offices designated for this purpose. Of the respondents, 50 percent did have specific arms of the development or alumni offices or separate offices that engage alumni of color. We also asked respondents how many people of color work in their development and alumni relations divisions. Roughly 50 percent of the institutions had staffs boasting almost 13 percent employees of color. Unfortunately, many of these individuals are in-clerical and administrative roles. Most are not working as front-line fundraisers. The other respondents had between one and three people of color working in development. Having few people of color makes it nearly impossible to engage alumni of color on a comprehensive level.

We were also interested in the ways in which institutions communicate with their alumni of color and whether or not this communication was separate from other alumni communication. Ninety percent of the institutions surveyed do not have separate publications for alumni of color, choosing instead to use their mainstream alumni publications to tap into the alumni of color population. This strategy is particularly problematic because alumni of color tend to fall through the cracks in mainstream publications, appearing for Black history month only or in stereotypical photos. Fortunately, there are good examples of institutions that do reach out specifically to alumni of color and these are highlighted in the next section of this chapter, which pertains to the interviews we conducted.

We interviewed a diverse group of majority institutions for this book. Almost all of these institutions are implementing some programs or practices that engage alumni of color. However, the Ivy League institutions that participated in this study were out in front in terms of their efforts to engage alumni of color. They have the longest history of engagement, alumni of color participation, and systemic programs aimed at soliciting alumni of color. They have considerably more resources and are directing some of them toward alumni and donors of color. In addition, the presidents of these institutions support the efforts of the office of institutional advancement and development, providing top-down support, which is important. These institutions also track their alumni of color, keeping records of their participation, their volunteerism, and their gift size. When asked, they can immediately tell you about the contributions of their alumni of color. Also of note, many of these schools have specific people assigned to work with their alumni of color initiatives. A few schools have several individuals dedicated to this work.

Overall, even among the non-Ivy League schools we interviewed, the institutions that were most successful had designated individuals working in both development and alumni relations. Having a dedicated staff member shows a firm commitment to engaging alumni of color. In most cases, the initiatives related to alumni of color were started by alumni groups that wanted to be more involved, but were finding it difficult to participate in the traditional activities offered by their alma maters.

The most successful institutions were those that involved alumni of color in many areas within their institution. Alumni felt valued and were more likely to continue their involvement. In addition, the successful institutions did not operate with a "one size fits all" approach to fundraising. They employ both targeted strategies for alumni of color and they fold these approaches into the general strategies for engaging all alumni. Successful institutions find that targeted marketing, solicitation, and communication garners better and more consistent results with alumni of color. Lastly, the most successful institutions connected students of color activities on campus with alumni of color activities. They worked to bring students and alumni together in an effort to engage the alumni and make career and mentoring connections for the students.

It is important to note that we did interview institutions that had no programs at all for engaging alumni of color. The lack of program sends a message that the institutions do not care.

CAMPUS CULTURE SHAPES ALUMNI GIVING

Those institutions that have the strongest programs or efforts for engaging alumni of color are also those who put effort into diversifying their campuses. For example, at Emory University, entering students of color are matched with mentors from the junior and senior classes to help smooth their transition to campus (personal communication, Emory University development staff, 2011). According to a staff member at Emory:

> We have a mentor program, which is a freshman program matching underrepresented students with upper class students. Roughly, 120 first year students sign up for this annually and we have over 70 upper class students who mentor them. Through monthly activities they meet as a family, which means that they meet beyond their one-on-one mentor/mentee pair. These families are very intentionally diverse so that students from different backgrounds interact with each other.
>
> (Donna Wong, Director of Multicultural Programs and Services)

In addition, faculty members of color are encouraged to mentor new students of color. These relationships are vital to alumni giving in the future as faculty members have some of the closest relationships with students on all college campuses.

At Brown University, all students are encouraged to participate in programs sponsored by the Third World Transition Program, which began in the 1960s and has bolstered the lives of students of color for decades (personal communication,

Brown University development staff, 2011). And, at the University of North Carolina, Chapel Hill, both students and alumni make considerable use of the institution's cultural centers, considering them a safe haven within the larger institution. According to one development officer at the University of North Carolina, Chapel Hill, "We have a black cultural center, an American Indian Center and a Latino initiative on our campus."

As we have mentioned throughout this book, the demographics of the country are rapidly changing and colleges and universities will no longer have a choice as to whether or not to engage all of their alumni. In order to survive and flourish, they will have to begin to pay attention to this important group. Many of the institutions that we talked to are already using replicable strategies to engage alumni of color.

STAFF SUPPORT FOR ALUMNI OF COLOR

As noted earlier in this chapter, some of the institutions in the Association of American Universities group have people of color working in the development and alumni relations areas although the numbers are still considerably small. We were interested in learning more about those institutions that have positions that focus specifically or in part on alumni of color. During our interviews, we asked about these positions. Three institutions stand out in terms of being exemplars with their attention on alumni of color as demonstrated through staffing. At Brown University, one person targets alumni of color in institutional advancement. This individual is the Director of Regional and Multicultural Programs and works with all race-specific and regional affinity groups. Brown has major alumni groups for its Black, Latino, and Asian alumni and the designated staff members interact with these affinity groups on a consistent and regular basis. Although Emory University does not have a dedicated person that works with alumni of color, the institution has regional development officers who are assigned to work with the various alumni of color chapters and to help coordinate their events (personal communication, Emory University development staff, 2011).

At Cornell University, the student population has become much more diverse and the development and alumni relations staff has realized that this increased diversity is leading to increased diversity amongst the alumni (personal communication, Cornell University development staff, 2011). According to one development office at Cornell:

> Students of color make up about a third of the undergraduate population . . . and about 20 percent of the population of the grad and professional students is also students of color. If you look back at the 70's and compare it to now, the university is a very, very different place than it was 40 years ago, or 45 years ago, when it was predominantly white and male . . . I think what has happened over the years is that Cornell has become a lot more representative of what the United States population looks like.
> (Richard Bank, Associate Vice President Alumni Affairs & Development Administration)

Cornell now has two full-time staff members working with alumni of color and, in fact, one of these individuals has been in place for the past 15 years, showing a commitment to engaging the alumni of color population on the institution's part. Through these positions, as well as the rest of the staff, Cornell is able to target all of the alumni of color. The main strategy for doing so is to engage the affinity groups to which they belong. The staff members guide the groups, but give them a lot of autonomy in terms of their leadership and programming. Cornell has alumni affinity groups for Blacks, Latinos, and Asians (personal communication, Cornell University development staff, 2011). In the words of one development officer at Cornell, "We made a decision to start programming specifically towards alumni of color in the 1990s. But, we're heavily volunteer-driven and we look for people to sort of create their own alumni groups, with our help, of course. All of our groups are very happy."

Of note, the institutional advancement and alumni affairs leadership at Cornell has been working to diversify its fund-raising staff. This is not the message that we heard from the majority of institutions in either our interviews or the surveys. Of course some institutions were adding positions and were aware of their shortfalls in terms of staffing, but many institutions either had not thought of staff diversity as an asset or do not understand the connection between a diverse staff and engaging alumni of color. According to the development staff at Cornell, they had to make a conscious effort to diversify their staff because of where the institution is located – in Ithaca, New York. In addition to diversifying the demographics at the institution, Cornell is also trying to increase the cultural competency of its current staff through workshops, reading, and training. According to one of the leaders in development at Cornell:

> What we're trying to do, ultimately, is to have a more diverse workplace. It is a challenge here in a place like Ithaca, because the population is what it is here, and we have to bring so many people in from the outside. But, we need to be more diverse . . . to ensure we are relevant to our alumni body on a sustainable basis . . . that's a big deal for us, and we are paying attention to that.
>
> (Richard Bank, Associate Vice President Alumni Affairs & Development Administration)

An institution that is quite unique among the colleges and universities that we interviewed and surveyed is the University of Washington. It is unique because of its large Native American student and alumni population. In order to engage this population as well as the rest of its alumni of color, the University of Washington alumni and development staff started a group 15 years ago called the Multicultural Alumni Partnership (MAP) to raise funds for scholarships for students of color. In order to avoid being considered in violation of the state's anti-affirmative action laws, MAP is a separate entity from the university – although it is housed in the alumni association. As a separate charitable organization, MAP can offer race-based scholarships to students (personal communication, University of Washington diversity office staff, 2011). According to a staff member in the diversity office:

> The scholarships are race-specific, so it's not the broader definition of diversity. It's a coalition of African-American, Asian American, Native American, and Latino alumni who are doing this work, and that's who they give the scholarships to. Each year MAP holds a major breakfast where we bring about five to six hundred alumni and community people together to talk about what is happening relative to diversity at the University of Washington. My development team helps them put on the breakfast, manage and steward their donations.
>
> (Shelia E. Lange, Vice President/
> Vice Provost Minority Affairs & Diversity)

In an effort to engage the Native American population specifically, the university sponsors tribal summits that are aimed at recruiting and retaining Native American students. Alumni take part in these summits. The institution's president is fully engaged in this initiative (personal communication, University of Washington diversity office staff, 2011). In addition, the institution sponsors programs in which current students engage tribal communities with students describing their experiences on campus. In the words of one staff member at the University of Washington:

> Our president and regents actually started hosting a tribal leadership summit, where we bring tribal chairs to campus once a year to talk about what we're doing relative to student recruitment and retention, faculty recruitment and retention, and research partnerships. So, it hasn't necessarily translated into large donations, but we are now routinely getting $10,000 from individual tribes, whereas before they would not.

They would give directly to student groups, but they would not give funds to the university.

(Shelia E. Lange, Vice President/
Vice Provost Minority Affairs & Diversity)

Likewise, faculty members have done cooperative research with tribal communities using alumni connections to facilitate appropriate research. The results of these efforts are significant in that the Native American alumni population now gives to mainstream causes at the institution rather than only Native American-oriented causes. One of the main reasons why the efforts at the University of Washington are successful is that the office of diversity is fully engaged with the office of institutional advancement and alumni affairs. The two parts of the campus work together to connect students and alumni.

At the University of North Carolina, Chapel Hill there are two positions within development and alumni relations that are specifically focused on alumni of color. According to development staff, these positions came from the alumni. They did not see many alumni of color who were engaged in the university's most recent campaign and brought this to the attention of their administration. In the words of one University of North Carolina, Chapel Hill alumni staff member:

The alumni thought the institution was losing a great opportunity to both engage and solicit the growing body of alumni of color at UNC. Of note, instead of merely complaining about being left out of the conversation, the alumni took action and sought out ways to be involved. They pointed out that during the last campaign, there were missed opportunities for engaging minority alumni. When you looked at our ranks in terms of the volunteer support we were not well represented in the volunteer structure for the campaign or other permanent campus committees. So this group, about five of them, brought the idea to the powers that be here and said we really think this is a real opportunity and we need to tap into this in terms of financial support.

(Jackie Pierce, Major Gifts Officer for Diverse Constituencies)

As we are writing this book there is growing contention around racial issues throughout the nation. Much of this animosity and strife has taken place in California and has resulted in Proposition 209, which limits the use of race in any way within the higher education system. For example, race cannot be considered in admissions, data collection related to students, or work with alumni. Proposition 209 has placed the public institutions in California under significant constraints as it pertains to understanding its alumni population. The universities that we interviewed have to be creative in their approach to working with alumni of color. For example, at the University of California, Berkeley, there is the California alumni association, which is separate from the institution. They are able to award race-based scholarships to high-achieving, low-income families. In addition to these scholarships, Berkeley has alumni clubs that are based on race and ethnicity and volunteers lead them. The university does have a division of equity and inclusion and this organization actively fundraises with diverse alumni. Alumni of color and the Berkeley community are very upset about Proposition 209. For example, the institution would like to launch a fundraising campaign for students of color but the university cannot truly engage. Alumni of color are frustrated and do not think the university wants them. Despite Proposition 209, Berkeley has been able to engage some of its alumni. However, we wonder how much more the institution could do without the constraints of Proposition 209, which not only limits the diversity on campus but also the engagement of these alumni of color. Like Berkeley, the University of California, Los Angeles (UCLA) is under the same constraints. UCLA also cleverly circumvents the confines of Proposition 209 by hiring a highly diverse staff. In fact, the 61 people on the development and alumni relations staff speak 21 different languages. Having a diverse staff in myriad ways results in the ability to engage alumni of color even though there is not a dedicated position.

UNDERSTANDING THE REPRESENTATION OF
ALUMNI OF COLOR

One of the chief problems on majority campuses is that there is little to no understanding of alumni of color and their representation within the overall alumni. During our interviews and surveying, we found that the majority of institutions had no formal mechanism for capturing alumni of color representation and some institutions had not considered the question. Some institutions are in a catch 22: they cannot make a convincing argument to administrators to dedicate more money and positions to engaging and soliciting alumni of color because they do not have the data to show that these alumni are active and worth engaging. This problem perpetuates the fallacy that alumni of color do not give because there is no data available to show otherwise.

Knowing the breakdown, in terms of representation of alumni of color, is essential to engaging this population and the future of fundraising. Some of the institutions with whom we talked are out in front and leading the way on engagement of alumni of color. They know the demographic make-up of their alumni. For example, at Brown University in Providence, Rhode Island, alumni of color represent 11,000 members of their alumni. Asian Americans and Pacific Islanders make up the largest group of alumni of color, then Blacks, Latinos and Native Americans respectively. At Emory University, 14 percent of the alumni are of color. The institution uses ethnicity codes in their alumni database in order to track the growing alumni of color population. At Cornell University, 13 percent of the alumni are of color and more specifically 3 percent are Black, 7 percent are Asian, 2 percent are Latino, and 1 percent are Native American. The University of North Carolina, Chapel Hill also tracks its alumni of color, noting that 13 percent of the alumni belong to this category. Of note, UC-Berkeley and other public institutions in California are not allowed to collect racial and ethnic data.

Despite these constraints, the institution estimates that roughly 15 percent of its alumni are alumni of color, with that percentage heavily skewed toward the last 20 years given the lack of diversity during the institution's early years.

Having an understanding of the representation of alumni of color is a first step to acknowledging their presence and the contributions that they can make if properly engaged in the institution. In future years, institutions will also need to consider bi-racial and multi-racial alumni as interracial marriage is on the rise and these alumni may report participation in multiple racial categories.

In addition to the presence of alumni of color, institutions need to collect information on the giving levels of these constituents. Unfortunately, most of the AAU institutions with whom we talked are not aware of alumni of color giving in any substantial way. Of those who are capturing alumni of color giving, Emory, Cornell, and the University of North Carolina, Chapel Hill reported some of the highest giving levels among their communities of color. Not only do these institutions track their alumni, but they correlate the presence of alumni with the giving. Of note, those institutions with the highest level of alumni of color giving have a staff member assigned to work specifically with these groups. They also have a diverse group of programs to engage these alumni. There is a direct connection between institutional success and the effort put into alumni of color initiatives. At Emory University, for example, the giving rate among alumni of color is 35 percent as compared to 50 percent among alumni overall. The average size gift among alumni of color is $136.55 compared to $477.93 for the overall alumni base (personal communication, Emory University development staff, 2011). At Cornell University, the development and alumni relations staff members focus on participation rates rather than the overall gift amount. Cornell looks at the raw numbers because when one looks at the size of the gift, it presents a false reading of alumni giving. For example, most of the alumni of color are younger and younger people give smaller gifts whereas majority alumni are older and older alumni give larger gifts. Moreover, older alumni members are often male and men have access to more income and assets, which results in larger gifts. It is vital that issues of age and gender among alumni cohorts are considered when reporting alumni of color giving data. At Cornell, 12 percent of Black alumni were donors. This is compared to only 3 percent in 1999. Through greater engagement, the institution has been able to increase its giving among African American donors substantially. In particular, Cornell encourages participation among younger alumni while focusing on increasing gift size among older alumni. Asian and Hispanic alumni both give at a rate of 11 percent, which is up from 2 percent in 1999. And Native Americans give at a rate of 12 percent, which has increased since 1999 when the rate was 9 percent. Of importance in the Cornell example is that the institution is tracking giving over time. This allows them to create momentum among the alumni of color groups as well as the upper level administration, making it easier to craft an argument for more institutional support to further engagement.

At the University of North Carolina, Chapel Hill, giving among alumni of color is roughly 10 percent, whereas overall giving is at 21 percent. The alumni and development staff members credit the cultural centers on campus for being a galvanizing force in the institution's ability to engage alumni of color. Cultural centers offer safe spaces on majority campuses and often support both the intellectual and social needs of students of color (Patton, 2010). In addition, those at UNC note that the institution's leadership is behind the alumni of color initiative and that this has led to its success. They also caution other institutions with regard to giving up on initiatives after only a short time, noting that these alumni of color initiatives take time and you have to wait three or four years to watch them take on a life of their own.

COMMUNICATION TOOLS FOR REACHING OUT
TO ALUMNI OF COLOR

Those institutions with the most success in terms of engaging and soliciting their alumni have specific communication tools for use with them. These communication tools fall into two categories: public relations and programs. The most successful institutions have direct mail programs with specific pieces for the various alumni groups. These pieces are most often segmented by race and ethnicity, as efforts to lump all alumni of color together are not often successful. The group that objects to this most often is the Asian American alumni. They prefer to be engaged as Asians alone or as a subgroup of the Asian population, such as Indian or Chinese. At Brown University, faculty and students of color co-sign direct mail pieces with alumni of color. Most successful institutions feature alumni of color in their mainstream publications, but also aim specific publications at the various alumni of color groups.

Alumni of color respond well to web-based representations of their needs and experiences. Many of the institutions that we communicated with have extensive websites, highlighting their alumni of color efforts. These institutions also have a substantial Facebook and Twitter presence. They use these social media sites to inform, celebrate, and highlight activities and accomplishments of alumni of color and students of color on the campus. Emory University is considerably out in front with regard to social media, employing a social media specialist who maintains and manages the institution's development and alumni relations presence on social media. Alumni are able to have direct and immediate interaction with the institution and they are also able to express their concerns and appreciation. According to an advancement staff member at Emory:

> We rely heavily on social media for all of our communications with all of our alumni groups. It's a really big part of the alumni association and our

strategy helps us get people at events. It also gets the brand out there. Also, it's a good way of finding out what alumni are doing and for them to hear from us as well.

(Donna Wong, Director of Multicultural Programs and Services)

At Brown University, African American alumni were inspired by the well-publicized example of its president Ruth Simmons. Simmons is the first and only African American president of an Ivy League institution. She made a leadership gift of $50,000 and this was the impetus for a large increase in giving among Black alumni (personal communication, Brown University development staff, 2011). The institution publicized Simmons' gift to alumni through various outlets.

The University of North Carolina, Chapel Hill fosters a very strong presence for alumni of color on the university website – it highlights all the alumni of color initiatives. The institution also publishes an electronic newsletter twice a year, which is sent to 18,000 alumni of color. The development and alumni relations offices are active on Facebook, hosting the "Celebrating Carolina's Diversity" page, which attracts many alumni of color. The University of North Carolina, Chapel Hill also works hard to make sure that their marketing materials have representation from all racial and ethnic groups so that everyone feels included. In addition, they measure the success of their solicitations. According to a member of the alumni relations staff:

We make sure that we have enough alumni and students of color represented whether on our website, communication pieces or our annual report. All of our marketing materials are reflective of the cultures that are found here at the university.

(Ronda Manuel, Director of Diversity in Annual Giving)

Penn State has a development committee that is diverse and advises the staff on alumni of color issues. This committee has helped develop a case statement for educational equity, which is shared with various constituents of the institution. However, this statement is not strictly race-based. It also focuses on low-income, underrepresented alumni.

PROGRAMS THAT FOSTER COMMUNICATION

Brown University uses its alumni affinity groups to communicate with alumni and to build a strong alumni base. In fact, the institution encourages students of color to join these groups while students in order to cultivate future givers. Emory University also uses its affinity groups to bolster alumni of color interest. Although the institution does not dictate the activities of the affinity groups, it does give them funding, which fosters activity and engagement on the part of the alumni. In addition, Emory works through the Caucus of Emory Black Alumni (CEBA), a black alumni organization, and matches current students with CEBA members in professions of interest to them. The CEBA members mentor students and as a result feel engaged with the institution and valued as alumni. CEBA is also tapped when Emory is looking for potential board of trustee members. This strategy is particularly important because Emory is able to achieve diversity in terms of the people who are chosen for board positions rather than tapping the same people over and over, which is a significant problem at most institutions. In addition to mentoring and board service, CEBA is heavily involved with recruitment and retention, networking, and professional development. The idea for CEBA spawned out of an alumni group rather than the university but, nonetheless, it has been quite successful.

There is some evidence that alumni of color from the 1960s and 1970s are more comfortable assimilating into the larger alumni population whereas younger alumni prefer to be identified by their ethnicity. It is important to understand an institution's unique alumni population and how the various segments prefer to be identified. At Brown University, they survey alumni to help understand their preferences for engagement and activity. This strategy enables them to better serve their alumni of color. According to a member of the Brown advancement staff:

> We sent a survey out to all Brown self-identified alumni of color, asking them what were some of the issues or areas they would like to support at Brown, outside of the Brown Annual Fund. The results of that survey became the focus areas for our Alumni of Color Initiative. Within that initiative, it was very clear that each of those communities, the African-American community, the Latino community, the Asian community and the multiracial and Native American alumni wanted to support endowed scholarships for students, so we actually set goals of creating endowments. We set goals for $250,000 endowments, named for these alumni affinity groups for students of color.
>
> (Suzy Alba, Assistant Director of Annual Giving)

UC-Berkeley is not allowed to use targeted marketing because of Proposition 209 and constraints on asking for race-specific data. Instead, they work through their Black, Latino, and Native American alumni groups. Through these groups, they can get the names of alumni of color and market to them but this is quite limited.

Cornell has done away with printed communications and instead does all of its publishing online. All of the communications are representative of the diversity on campus. They make a concerted effort to be inclusive of all alumni in all situations. Cornell has a 20-year history of engaging alumni of color and today those groups are producing alumni leaders that are taking on larger roles at the institution such as joining the board of trustees and the president's council of women. Alumni of color are also participating in the capital campaign and working on raising money for scholarships for students of color. Because Cornell has engaged alumni of color for so long, these individuals are becoming ambassadors for the entire institution and not just alumni of color. Many of the institution's strongest and most visible leaders now come from these affinity groups. Cornell's success in terms of engaging alumni of color demonstrates that if you ask people to participate and give them something meaningful to do, they are happy to help and step up to leadership positions (personal communication, Cornell University development staff, 2011). Of note, the initial impetus for engaging alumni of color came from the top, but now the entire institution is willing to "listen and learn" (personal communication, Cornell University development staff, 2011). According to advancement staff at Cornell:

> If you don't have the leaders of the organization making a public commitment to engaging diverse students, diverse alumni, then you won't have a commitment. It also requires a team of people, both volunteers and staff, to be open to what that opportunity represents. I think that Cornelians believe that we're a stronger place, a better organization, for having a more diverse population. Support has to come from the top. But there also has to be a culture that allows this support, or even facilitates these kinds of opportunities to present themselves.
>
> (James Mazza, Assistant Vice President Alumni Affairs and Development)

The development and alumni relations staff members capitalize on the openness to working with alumni of color that has permeated the institution. For example, each of the colleges is charged with increasing participation among alumni of color. As evidence of its commitment to working with alumni of color and making this work a priority in the institution, they hired a person specifically for this job. She works centrally and with all the schools on campus and because alumni affairs and development are fully integrated on Cornell's campus, working relationships are almost seamless. This new position is focused on engaging alumni of color, which is a primary goal of Cornell's development and alumni relations staff. They think it is vital to engage these alumni sufficiently before considering solicitation.

Alumni of color have not always had the best relationships with their predominantly White alma maters and, as such, spending time engaging is important to fundraising success.

In an effort to ensure future success at the institution, Cornell alumni relations staff members are beginning to teach students to be philanthropic, including students of color. The institution would like to have the same success with students of color that it is having with alumni of color, making for a smooth transition as these students become alumni (personal communication, Cornell University development staff, 2011). The institution also has a MOSAIC program in which minority alumni take leadership roles. These alumni of color do signature events – two or three a year – that bring together diverse groups, majority alumni, and students on campus. The events are attended by large numbers of students of color.

The University of Washington hosts a breakfast and tailgate at homecoming specifically for alumni of color. Afterwards, alumni attend the football game together. The institution uses homecoming as a way to bring alumni of color together and reignite their passion and commitment for the institution.

The University of North Carolina, Chapel Hill sponsors a Black alumni reunion, which started with a few members of the alumni over a decade ago and now attracts over 1,200 people annually (personal communication, University of North Carolina development staff, 2011). The institution also has Native American and Latino alumni reunions. Alumni of color drive these events with the help of the general alumni association. They are given a lot of autonomy in order to encourage ownership of the activities. Through their extensive work and relationship building with alumni of color, the alumni and development staff at UNC has discovered that with alumni of color, giving has to be tied to something concrete. Alumni of color, by and large, do not want to give to ambiguous things or causes; endowments are particularly difficult (personal communication, University of North Carolina development staff, 2011).

At UCLA, there are 104 affinity groups, many which are race-based and others that are professional or academic. Increased diversity in the state and among the student body is going to shift the alumni base going forward. The UCLA alumni and development staff is aware that their approach will have to change. All of the affinity groups do fundraising especially in the area of scholarships. Due to Proposition 209, the affinity groups funnel their money through an external foundation, which awards scholarships bases on race and ethnicity.

At Texas A&M University, the alumni and development staff work with students of color to write to alumni of color within the various schools. There has been a push for academic units, other than just student affairs, to reach out to students of color.

Although there is considerable work that needs to be done in terms of engaging alumni of color at majority institutions, we have identified some best practices at colleges and universities throughout the nation. These best practices can be learned from and adopted on your institution's campus.

7

A CONVERSATION WITH ALUMNI OF COLOR

Thus far, we have talked about the perspectives of alumni relations and development officers at majority institutions as well as the history and traditions of giving within various communities of color. In trying to gain a better understanding of the motivations and perspectives of alumni of color, we surveyed alumni of color from majority institutions throughout the country. Through the voices and perspectives of these alumni, we learned their reasons for giving (or not giving) and volunteering (or not volunteering).

WHY THEY GIVE

Majority alumni give for a variety of well-documented reasons. They give if they have an emotional connection to the cause. For example, if they are breast cancer survivors or if someone in their family is, they will give to breast cancer research or a teaching hospital. They also give because of feelings of guilt or empathy. For example, perhaps they did something that they regret in their youth and now they want to give to programs that prevent such behavior. Like some alumni of color, majority alumni give out of a sense of obligation – someone did something for them and now they will return the favor to someone else. However, the main difference here is that the sense of obligation is not to their specific race or ethnic group in all cases. Majority alumni are more likely to give if they feel socially pressured by their friends or pressure to keep up with their friends' philanthropic giving. And lastly, majority alumni are often motivated to give by the prospect of notoriety (e.g. they want their name on a building).

With regard to making monetary contributions to their alma mater, there were four major reasons why alumni of color gave and gave regularly: obligation, continuing university traditions, supporting students, and fostering diversity. First, many alumni of color felt obligated to give back to their alma mater because of the life-changing and influential experiences that took place during their college years. For example, one African American alumnus stated, "My alma mater was a wonderfully enriching experience. I donate what I can even though I am currently in graduate school and living on loans. I realize that even $10 a year helps boost the overall alumni donation rate, which schools rely on for rankings." Likewise, an Asian American alumnus said, "I believe that it's important to provide financial support for my alma mater for two reasons: I was supported in that way as an undergraduate and I recognize that it's a part of some measures of educational quality." A Latina alumna was deeply passionate about her obligation to give back, which she said stems from the benefits she received from her alma mater: "I gained so many benefits from attending the institution and part of it was due to the alumni and their gifts to us students. I feel an obligation to give back." Among alumni of color, being asked is essential to giving and increased giving. One alumnus personified this idea, stating "They asked and a sense of obligation made me contribute. The social, educational, and professional experiences I had as an undergraduate not only helped me to make life-long friends who cared about me but it shaped all of my future experiences."

Another important reason for giving back that alumni of color noted frequently was an interest in supporting current students. Alumni wanted to provide an experience to future students much like the one they had. According to a Latino alumnus, "I would like to assist in making a remarkable experience for the generations to come. My contributions help with educational opportunities and promote the ultimate college experience." One African American alumna was very specific in her contributions, wanting them to go directly toward programs that foster student success. She said, "I donate yearly to my alma mater's library, asking that they purchase books and other educational materials that can be used to help students strive for student success. Students need skills to overcome adversity." A Native American student said, "Giving back is the right thing to do. I remember that there were things lacking at my alma mater when I was a student and I don't want the next students to have that experience. I want them to have a great experience."

A third reason for giving among alumni of color is a commitment to the university traditions and the idea of continuing these traditions. One Black alumnus said, "Although the institution has its faults, I value the mission and vision of the institution. I want my degree to mean something in 30 years and I need to play a part in supporting the institution to make this reality." For those alumni of color who had positive experiences, they wanted to ensure that the traditions that led them to succeed remain on campus. They saw these traditions as community building.

The last major reason why alumni of color gave back to their alma maters pertained to the support of diversity and diversity related efforts. One Latina alumna explained, "I believe that my alma mater encompassed the foundation for my career with a sound academic curriculum, developed each student to reach their professional potential through engaging projects, community involvement, corporate interactions, accredited programs, knowing that the student was the benefactor. It did all of this while demonstrating a commitment to diversity and an infrastructure that supported it." One Black alumnus created an emergency fund for students of color. He had "things pop up" in college and knew that students of color need a safety net.

WHY THEY VOLUNTEER

Alumni of color volunteered for three main reasons: to mentor students, to be active in social events, and to serve on committees and boards. Mentoring students as well as talking to prospective students were common reasons why alumni wanted to get involved. Alumni often expressed interest in "coming back to mentor students" or "helping to counsel high school students considering their alma mater." They were particularly interested in interacting with potential students of color and encouraging them to attend their alma maters. Of note, they think that students of color need to know that others have gone before them and that students of color are more likely to enroll if they meet with alumni of color. A Latino alumnus regularly participates in speaking engagements at his alma mater's homecoming events. He likes to be "accessible to undergraduate students." Countless alumni of color serve as readers for scholarship competitions and admissions processes. They enjoyed these activities and felt much more connected to the institution when they participated in this way. Individuals claimed they were "making an impact" on the institution through these types of volunteerism – a tangible, concrete impact.

Many alumni of color belong to social organizations focused on their race or culture. Those we surveyed were interested in volunteering with these organizations. One Black male alumnus said, "I like to volunteer with organizations that shaped me while I was in college. One organization, in particular, was focused on community service and multiple racial communities benefited from their work. I like going back and working with them." In addition to an interest in working with specific organization that they used to belong to, the alumni of color enjoy participating in college- and university-sponsored activities that reach out to racial and ethnic minorities in the surrounding communities. However, they are not interested in activities that patronize "Black and Brown communities." Instead, they want to see their alma maters reach out to communities surrounding campus and uplift these communities, making meaningful change.

Another way that alumni of color were involved is on alumni committees and boards but this was minimal and concentrated at only a few institutions. Some alumni chose to serve on boards specifically related to alumni of color or women. They were also active in young alumni associations, which tended to have more alumni of color and engaged them more fully. Making the transition to the general alumni boards was difficult as these are typically majority White and not as inclusive. The alumni's reporting of their activity is consistent with what we learned about the majority institutions that participated in this study. By and large, only a few institutions have extensive opportunities and outreach with alumni of color.

WHY THEY DON'T GIVE

Alumni of color had myriad reasons for not giving. Some of these are in line with those of majority alumni, including not being asked, not understanding the needs of the institution, and not knowing how. However, their other reasons were somewhat unique and often troubling. The most common reason for not giving back to their alma mater was that they were not asked or informed about giving and felt that there was a lack of communication on the part of the institution. As we have mentioned throughout this book, people of color are rarely seen as givers and instead tend to be looked upon as receivers of philanthropy by majority institutions. Alumni of color can sense these kinds of perceptions and they act as a deterrent to giving.

Another common reason why alumni of color do not give back is that they had "poor" college and university experiences, in which they felt marginalized and ostracized by their alma mater. Some alumni of color told us that they "don't have confidence in the administration" and do not feel that there is "sincerity" toward them and their inclusion in the institution. One Latino alumnus said, "I do not actively donate to my alma mater because of the racism and lack of inclusion I experienced while an undergraduate." Alumni of color often feel disconnected or a lack of affinity toward their alma mater because of their experiences.

Given that many alumni of color grow up in low-income families, they are often disinclined to give to their alma maters if the institutions are heavily endowed. And, what makes matters worse is that the institutions rarely explain how fundraising and philanthropy work to alumni of color so their attitudes are not easily changed. In order to change perceptions, institutions need to reach out to alumni of color regularly. One Asian American alumnus told us, "My alma mater has so much money that I feel like anything I contribute would not even be appreciated." This statement is troubling because it makes it clear that the individual is not being engaged and does not understand how valuable alumni contributions are in terms of demonstrating support to foundations and corporate funders. Yet another alumna – this time an African American female – exclaimed, "I do not regularly donate because I feel like my alma mater is a powerhouse and that they have more money than they will ever know what to do with. In addition, the issues I feel passionate about are not important to the institution." Sometimes an alumnus of color will give regardless of their sense of the institution's overwhelming wealth. Nearly 40 percent of our survey respondents were willing to give to their wealthy alma maters if the funds went directly to students. According to one Native American alumnus, "My alma mater has an abundance of rich, white donors that support the school. I would much rather support the students, especially other Native American students, and feel like I am making an impact on them."

Institutional wealth as a hindrance to giving is common among alumni of color, with many of them expressing frustration over the larger percentage of merit aid being awarded to students who already have great wealth. Most elite majority institutions are fighting over a select group of students and, in order to lure them to their institutions, they offer large merit aid packages regardless of financial need. This practice maintains a steady flow of affluent students but results in very few low-income students. At elite majority institutions the number of students with Pell Grants is dismal, hovering at around 7–8 percent. Alumni of color are aware of this and deeply frustrated with the situation. In the words of one alumnus, "Stop doling out millions in merit aid and actually have a commitment to serving marginalized students."

Another misconception about giving to higher education pertained to "not knowing where the money is going." Alumni of color are deeply concerned with how their contributions are being used and where they are being applied. When this is not being communicated regularly and in a timely manner, alumni of color tend to refrain from giving. As mentioned, most racial and ethnic minorities want to give to tangible and concrete causes.

The final reason that some alumni of color do not give is that they are not financially stable after graduation, and sometimes for almost a decade. Due to racial inequality in the United States, people of color have less access to wealth and assets and as such are not able to give at the same levels as majority college graduates. Regardless, an overwhelming number of the alumni of color that we surveyed who were less than 10 years out of college did give, even if it was a small amount.

WHY THEY DON'T VOLUNTEER

Alumni of color were very likely to volunteer at their alma mater when they were asked. Unfortunately, they were rarely asked. One Black alumnus said, "I do not volunteer with my alma mater because I have not been presented any opportunities to do so." Another Asian American alumnus makes the problem even clearer, "If I was knowledgeable about volunteer opportunities in my area, I probably would volunteer." In some cases, the alumni of color contacted the development office, hoping to volunteer, but their calls and emails were not returned. Some alumni of color doubt their alma mater's interest in having them volunteer. They do not feel welcome. For example, according to this Black female, "My alma mater has never emphasized the importance of volunteering. In fact, it does not have a sense of how I have evolved professionally and, therefore, I get the sense that it lacks any interest in my involvement." Another Latina alumna noted, "I do not feel any affinity. My sense of connection is gone and no one has worked to reconnect me to the institution."

Unfortunately, some alumni of color had unpleasant and scarring experiences at their alma maters that continue to prevent them from volunteering. One African American alumnus told us, "What keeps me away from my alma mater and from volunteering is the racism, sexism, and homophobia. Purely stated, dealing with a hostile campus climate and people's xenophobia and hatred is toxic and taxing on my spirit." Although this Black male's response was much stronger than that of most respondents, it was not the only comment about the social and academic climate at many majority institutions. In order to better engage alumni of color, the campus environment must change. Many alumni question their alma mater's commitment to low-income, students of color.

BEST PRACTICES FOR ENGAGEMENT

Although we offer ideas for engagement and solicitation throughout this book, we thought it would be interesting to look at the recommendations that the alumni of color we surveyed suggested and recommended for their own alma maters. First and foremost, alumni of color want to be solicited and engaged by other alumni of their own race or ethnicity. It is not absolutely necessary, but it puts most alumni of color at ease. And if not a person of their own race, they prefer to be approached by another person of color.

Use of Social Media

The majority of the alumni of color we surveyed, regardless of age, used social media to communicate with other alumni and to keep up with current events. They want to be kept informed by their alma mater and prefer that this communication come through email and social media such as Facebook, Twitter, and LinkedIn.

Alumni Magazines

Alumni of color also want to see themselves in fundraising publications and alumni magazines, urging institutions to "develop targeted outreach to attract alumni like me." According to a Native American alumnus, "In the monthly magazine, rarely do I see alumni of color profiled or mentioned. I would love to read about the great work of all alumni." Among the alumni of color surveyed, there were many comments pertaining to the representation of people of color in institutional publications. They feel left out and overlooked and urge institutions to be genuine and fair in their highlighting of accomplishments. Perhaps the best advice came from this Black alumnus:

> The alumni communications continually highlight the work of white faculty, students, and alumni. It would be nice to see stories about people of color and what they are doing. The stories don't have to be cast in a diversity light. Just tell the stories. Include us. Don't save the showcase of African Americans for February. Show them all throughout the year. And don't highlight them just because they are Black. Showcase them because they are good at what they do and have a great story to share. The same for all alumni, faculty, and staff of color. Stop putting us in a box and pulling us out only when it's convenient or provides a clear advantage. If you believe we are a part of the institution, then act like it!

A Commitment to Diversity

Alumni of color are watching their alma maters and looking for evidence of a strong commitment to diversity. They want fundraising and engagement materials to speak to their interests and to focus on students and faculty of color. They are interested in knowing how the campus is changing and what strategies are being used to cope with the changes and enhance the learning environment for students of color. One African American alumnus said, "Keep me updated on ways that the school is improving. Maintain a strong commitment to diversity, and tailor material to minority alumni." Alumni of color want their alma maters to pay attention and tailor solicitations to their interests rather than only the interests of the majority alumni. They also want to learn about opportunities to give back to students like them. A Latino alumnus stated, "My alma mater should let me know when there are opportunities to give back to students of color, for example, scholarships, or opportunities to support student groups to which I belonged." Being made aware of opportunities, especially those related specifically to the interests of the alumni of color, makes a difference. This is evidenced in the words of this Black female, "Two years ago, I attended an African American Alumni Reunion. It drew me back to campus for the first time in 28 years. Had there been a specific project or program for me to become involved in at the time, I would have been hooked. I don't recall that there was such a program. Being on campus, renewing those incredible friendships that life has pushed aside was intoxicating."

Explaining Missteps of the Past

Overall, alumni of color are looking for explanations when they have been mistreated in the past and for warmth on the part of their alma mater. A Latina alumna made this very clear when she said, "I think for starters, picking up the phone and calling would be incredibly helpful. Also putting me in contact with other alumni would be a powerful gesture. To truly get me on campus would take a simple gesture of asking for my help. At my alma mater there were several racist incidents and, if people were willing to openly discuss these matters, I would be on the next flight there to return and help others." Alumni of color want to be involved in both decision making and giving. Too often, they are overlooked when leaders are sought to serve on boards within alumni organizations. According to one Black alumnus, "If they want to count us in their charitable giving, they need to count us in their decision making as well."

8

MODEL PROGRAMS FOR ALUMNI OF COLOR

In order to provide examples to those reading this book, we scoured the Internet for model programs. There is no need to recreate the wheel as many institutions have created great programs that work. These programs have several things in common that serve as the primary reason for their inclusion in this book. First, these model programs can be implemented at most institutional types. Depending on an institution's current diversity initiatives in the fundraising area, these programs may only require slight adjustments in order to be fully functioning. Second, these model programs are mainly driven by alumni volunteers and, as such, less costly. The office of development need only provide guidance and basic resources. Third, these model programs engage all of the institution's constituents, including current students and faculty. For example, many of the programs include mentoring, networking professional develop-ment, and recruiting. These initiatives cut across the many facets of an institution. Fourth, these model programs encourage alumni to re-connect with their former classmates, sharing achievements and accomplishments. This strategy is key to enhancing engagement and helping alumni of color feel welcome on campus. And finally, many of these model programs allow alumni of color to connect with their alma mater at the entry point of their choice, giving them more ownership in the engagement process. All of these programs lead to increased volunteerism and financial engagement on the part of alumni of color.

CARNEGIE MELLON UNIVERSITY

The Carnegie Mellon Hispanic-Latino Association provides a mentorship program entitled "Mi Amigo," which involves both current students and alumni. The program gives participants the opportunity to network, engage, and receive useful information and advice. Alumni aim to mentor students through their duration at Carnegie Mellon while they purse students' personal and professional goals.

The Carnegie Mellon Alumni Association hosts the annual homecoming weekend. Homecoming is complete with a weekend of fun-filled events for current students and alumni. Events included in the festivities are meet-and-greets with older associations, awards ceremonies, and a free 30-and-over dinner and party. The weekend is capped off with a religious rededication, brunch, meeting to discuss business, and lastly a gathering for members of the alumni association.

COLUMBIA UNIVERSITY

Alumni attended the first reception hosted by The Asian Columbia Alumni Association (ACAA). The benefit and scholarship dinner was a fundraising event. The purpose was to raise monies from alumni and high-profile attendees. While adding to the association's endowment, they also sought to provide scholarships to aid in the recruitment of highly accredited Asian Scholars. The event was a formal black tie forum complete with awards for honorees and achievement.

The ACAA has developed the ACAA scholarship fund to serve undergraduate and graduate students and endorsements. Monies raised are added to financial aid packages and offered to students to help compete with other school attracting Asian students. These scholarships last four years and help ease students' concerns of financing their tuition through graduation. Also afforded to international graduate students explicitly, are grants to offset the cost of taking English as a Second Language courses. Lastly, once a year ACAA will host a fundraiser with alumni and supporters. They have set a goal to raise $1 million for a future endowment.

An Asian American conference was held by the ACAA to honor the Columbia 250. The purpose of the conference was to promote awareness and pride in being Asian. Panel discussions were held in which they discussed topics such as being Asian American and learned about different ethnic studies. Also highlighted during the conference was the topic of how Asian Americans are portrayed in popular media today. Lastly, there was a panel on science and Asians' and their rank in the world in fields like technology.

The Columbia Mentoring Initiative (CMI), which is an offset of The Alumni of Color Outreach Program, offers mentoring between freshmen, upperclassmen, and alumni. The program helps students to become more acclimated to the university. Mentors help students succeed, feel welcome, and be aware of themselves within the school. The CMI works with multiple organizations on campus to offer them holistic support from cultural groups. Activities include heritage month, dinners, leadership activities, symposiums, and career exploration among others.

A scholarship fund operated by the Black Alumni Council raises money for students who attend the regular academic year as well as the summer. The purpose is to help relieve some financial stress for students who have trouble affording Columbia. For the traditional year they aim to provide five students with $10,000 scholarships. For the summer semesters they aim to provide two students $3,500.

CORNELL UNIVERSITY

In 2012 the Cornell Asian Alumni Association (CAAA) hosted a Pan Asian Banquet. Their mission was to raise $40,000 for students that meet specified criteria. The CAAA aims to develop strong relationships with former alumni, community leaders, and current students. They also promote honor in their heritage while collaborating with other Asian centered organizations.

The CAAA sponsors multiple Asian–Pacific American programs. They support career developments, networking, fundraisers, social gatherings, alumni book signings, dinners, and community services. In an effort to promote and recruit top Asian American students they partner and support the admissions department with scholarships. In an effort to show support of heritage and engage Native American students Cornell celebrated the foundation Akwe:kon. Speakers from the Native American community joined in the celebration. Akwe:kon sought to ensure added recruitment and allocation of resources to students of the community. They also wanted students to feel included instead of unwelcome.

As part of Cornell's efforts of outreach, the American Indian Program seeks to keep its tradition of giving back by participating in workdays at the Cayuga Share Farm. Volunteers work side by side with residents from the Cayuga Nation while picking fruits and engaging in dance. In addition, they tutor, mentor, and lead Native high school students weekly. The American Indian

Program provides scholarships for students in the archeology field. These scholarships provide funds for all tuition and living expenses for the summer course offered. The class and excavation takes place on property of the Iroquois Native people. Students receive lectures about the American Indian heritage and culture.

The 2012 Cornell Reunion, hosted by the Cornell Black Alumni Association (CBAA) serves as an opportunity for alumni to come together and celebrate past and recent achievements. They also provide scholarships to promote diversity on campus. The CBAA as an organization works together with the development staff and ultimately promotes giving back to the university.

The Cornell Black Alumni Association (CBAA) announced a new scholarship in honor of James and Janice Turner for over 90 years of service to Cornell. Janice Turner was the first director of the Africana Studies Center at Cornell. The CBAA gives money to African American scholars who want to attend the school.

EMORY UNIVERSITY

The Caucus of Emory Black Alumni (CEBA), through various modes, works to build meaningful relationships with its alumni, staff, faculty, and students. They act as a body that upholds the interest of African American alumni throughout the entire university. CEBA hosts and sponsors events such as social gatherings, volunteer projects, outreach, and musical forums.

HARVARD UNIVERSITY

Harvard Asian American Alumni Alliance (HAAAA) hosts an annual Global Leadership Reception for students and alumni. Friends, alumni, affiliated organizations, and universities around the world gather together for this event.

Harvard's Black Alumni Society hosts an alumni weekend. Close to 600 students, alumni, and faculty come together to enjoy a reunion packed with activities.

INDIANA UNIVERSITY

The Indiana University Latino Alumni Association (IULAA) financially supports qualified students who plan to benefit the Latino community or have an appreciation for Latino culture in the United States. The scholarship is granted to students who have high academic marks, exhibit leadership, and give back to their community.

JOHNS HOPKINS UNIVERSITY

The Society of Black Alumni in an effort to recruit prominent black scholars established an endowment (Presidential Professorship) to ensure funds are available to attract such professors.

MASSACHUSETTS INSTITUTE OF TECHNOLOGY (MIT)

Latino Alumni/ae of MIT (LAMIT) hosts a graduation luncheon to welcome new alumni of color. In addition, the Latino Alumni/ae of MIT (LAMIT) was awarded a Presidential Citation at the Lamit Ibero- Conference by the Ibero- American MIT Alumni Summit for showing the impact that international networks can have. They hosted a conference that had 60 representatives from nine different countries and brought distinguished Latino speakers to campus.

MICHIGAN STATE UNIVERSITY

MSU hosts a separate homecoming from its traditional all-inclusive one. The Black Alumni Homecoming includes a weekend complete with social events and alumni meetings.

NEW YORK UNIVERSITY

Established in October of 2009, the Multicultural Alumni Group supports undergraduates who demonstrate financial need and have a strong academic history. It is open to any student who is a member of an underrepresented minority on campus.

NORTHWESTERN UNIVERSITY

The Northwestern University Asian American Alumni club (NU-A5) hosts career networking with prominent speakers, wine tastings, art tours, and social events to engage its alumni. Nearly 20 percent of Northwestern's freshman class is either Asian or Asian American. Due to this higher than average percentage, the Northwestern Alumni Association recognized NU-A5 for its importance. Members of NU-A5 have access to employment opportunities, volunteer opportunities, reduced fees, and participation in the mentor/mentee program.

PRINCETON UNIVERSITY

The Princeton University Affiliated Group Dinner joins together the Asian American Alumni, Association of Black Princeton Alumni, Association of Latino Alumni, and The Princeton University Alumni to encourage unity and speak about engagement opportunities.

Princeton University offers the Princeton Prize in Race Relations to recognize students who are progressive in addressing racial harmony. The prize consists of 24 regional cash awards of $1,000. Winners are invited to take part in a two-day all-expense-paid symposium on race relations. During the symposium participants work on improving race relations in their respected communities as well as attend workshops and lecture series. Alumni are involved in this event.

PURDUE UNIVERSITY

The Purdue Black Alumni Organization provides scholarships to support African American and Latino students. Two highlighted scholarships are the Presidential Leadership Scholarship and Roger Blalock Scholarship. The Presidential scholarship was endowed in 1988 and is awarded to students based on academic achievement, leadership ability, and financial need. The Blalock scholarship, established in 2009, is awarded to one or two African American students with a minimum 2.8 GPA. The Latino Alumni Organization also holds award ceremonies, leadership conferences, and social gatherings.

RICE UNIVERSITY

Rice held three panel discussions to commemorate the 40th anniversary of the first African Americans to earn a bachelor's degree from their university. Included in their discussions were topics of discrimination, low numbers of Black enrollment, and future for minorities at Rice. One panel highlighted a period when Rice was segregated and discriminated against blacks. Another highlighted current students' experiences and recommendations for what Rice can and should do to recruit more students of color. The consensus of many in attendance is that Rice has come a long way compared to its past, but still has a long way to go in order to raise its Black enrollment from 6.3 percent.

RUTGERS UNIVERSITY

The Latino Alumni Association of Rutgers (LAARU) hosts many interactions to engage their alumni and students. For the fall semester there is the LAARU young alumni social, annual domestic violence awareness march and rally, and a leader's conference. One highlighted event is the alumni welcome to

Casa Abierta. This event involves starting off the year with an evening of dancing, eating, performances, and socializing. The leadership conference provides the opportunity for alumni relations to supply resources to leaders at Rutgers. There is also a reception recognizing alumni for their efforts in giving back. The goal for participants who attend any function is to make available resources for Rutgers future leaders.

STANFORD UNIVERSITY

The Stanford Chicano/Latino Alumni Association hosts its annual town hall. The town hall's purpose is to allow students the opportunity to hear about recent developments on and off campus.

The Stanford Asian American Alumni Club hosts multiple functions as a part of its purpose of engaging students. They have the Asian American activities center, town hall meetings, alumni panels with accomplished speakers, and various social/educational receptions. At all events students and community representatives are encouraged to meet and speak with alumni.

The Asian American Activities Center through its After Dark Series hosts a seminar to talk about dealing with financial pressures. Topics discussed include how to fit in when coming from low-income families and how to balance personal/academic interests while committing to financial pressures. The center also tackles the issue of dealing with parental pressures including choosing careers of their choice.

TEXAS A&M UNIVERSITY

The Committee for the Awareness of Mexican-American Culture hosts "Hola Day" as an effort to retain students. The goal is to get students involved with the campus and build a social/academic network. The committee also holds functions to celebrate Mexican culture through special festivities and recognition of cultural traditions. In addition to "Hola Day" the Memorial Student Center (MSC) invites the Hispanic student body to partake in other cultural celebrations such as Dia de los Muertos and Mis Quince Anos. These celebrations highlight those who have passed and a girls coming of age.

UNIVERSITY OF COLORADO

The Hispanic Alumni Association engages alumni through its annual Chile Open. The event raises money for Latino students. They also host an annual dinner dance fundraiser, which has raised over $950,000 since 1984.

The Black Alumni Association helps welcome incoming students and their families with their annual Summer Send Off. They encourage students to get involved and connected with all alumni young and old. The association acknowledges that African American students have trouble surviving at a predominantly White school and aims to assist Black students in succeeding at the University of Colorado.

UNIVERSITY OF CALIFORNIA-BERKELEY

The UC-Berkeley Chicano/Latino Alumni Association (CLAA) provides scholarships aimed at developing a supportive environment in which students continue learning while growing professionally. They also host social gatherings, fundraisers, and cultural events.

UNIVERSITY OF CALIFORNIA-DAVIS

The campus of UC Davis hosts Black Family Week to bring about awareness and celebrate the history of black culture on campus. During the week there are educational programs and the annual Delta Sigma Theta luncheon. In addition, activities for the week include wine socials, concerts, and varieties of food. Their main purpose is to give students and alumni an African Diaspora event to celebrate on campus.

Believed to be one of the largest student-run events in the nation, "Picnic Day" is celebrated as the flagship event in the UC system. "Picnic Day" recognizes diversity and achievement on campus and the community. Areas highlighted for achievement include research, teaching, and service. This event has been around since 1909 and continues with support from generous donations from various sources.

UNIVERSITY OF CALIFORNIA-IRVINE

The Vietnamese American Oral Project (VAOHP) at Irvine combines three years of efforts to preserve and promote the Vietnamese experience in Southern California. The project aims to grow the archives of Vietnamese Americans. In order to do so they acquire first-hand stories of Vietnamese people while their stories and experiences are still current.

UNIVERSITY OF CALIFORNIA-LOS ANGELES (UCLA)

UCLA's Filipino Alumni Network hosts its annual scholarship benefit that entails a VIP reception, silent auction, presentations, and awards.

The Latino Alumni Network brings together its alumni by enticing them with a holiday bash, art gallery, and Latin American art, culture, and cuisine. They enjoy Venezuelan food and drinks while viewing art. Also taking place at the event is a book drive benefitting a UCLA community school.

UNIVERSITY OF ILLINOIS

The university celebrates notable achievements of its alumni by posting alumni profiles online.

The Latina/o Alumni Association hosts an alumni networking function. Topics discussed at the event are post-college planning and learning how to talk professionally. The purpose is to help find mentors, seek guidance, and gain understanding. The association also provides book scholarships in the amount of $500 to undergraduate students.

UNIVERSITY OF KANSAS

The Black Alumni Chapter hosts its homecoming reunion weekend. The weekend includes events such as an alumni gala, fellowship services, and social gatherings. The weekend is meant to foster an environment in which black alumni network and reconnect themselves with the university.

The Hispanic Alumni Chapter hosts their reunion to gather with alumni for football and social gatherings. Their purpose is also to network and reconnect themselves with the university.

UNIVERSITY OF MARYLAND

The Asian Pacific American Alumni Association (AAST) host the Terps Walk for AAST. This fundraiser is a walk-a-thon that helps provide scholarships to Asian American students.

UNIVERSITY OF MICHIGAN

Alumni from the University of Michigan participate in minority recruiting events. Alumni socialize with prospective students to give them examples of their experiences while in school. They also answer any questions they may have about being a minority at a majority White school.

UNIVERSITY OF NORTH CAROLINA

The Alumni Committee on Racial and Ethnic Diversity hosts a forum on minority male achievement. They have experts in the subject speak about what can be done to increase success for students of color. The committee hopes to engage alumni and build stronger relationships with the university. Goals of their events also include responding to student appeals for support, examining current efforts, taking a strengths-based approach, and continuing the momentum already established across the campus.

UNIVERSITY OF PENNSYLVANIA

The Association of Native Alumni (ANA) acts as an advocate for Native American students on Penn's campus. They hold the interest of recruiting Native faculty, building friendships, and promoting Native interest.

The Penn Asian Alumni Network (UPAAN) hosts its annual mentoring exchange. The goal is to create an environment in which students and alumni gather to exchange resources, ideas, and mentors. They also aim to help participants explore possible career opportunities.

Penn also offers the Penn Spectrum conference and corresponding events, which focuses on bringing together alumni of color to talk about the ways that they want to be engaged in the university. Penn Spectrum brings together alumni on campus with administrative support to share cultural traditions and expertise.

UNIVERSITY OF ROCHESTER

The African American Network (AAN) invited the university community to partake in an evening of bowling. Their intent is to provide an opportunity for everyone to strengthen relationships, spend quality time, and meet new people. AAN hosts its annual family picnic as another way for the black community to come together. The goal of the events is to provide additional outlets for families and alumni to come together and network.

UNIVERSITY OF TEXAS AUSTIN

The Black Alumni Network works to engage both alumni and the community, promote black scholarships, and inform black students about resources available to them.

The Asian Alumni Association works to connect alumni, community, and celebrate Asian culture and heritage. They also provide resources and opportunities to Asian students.

UNIVERSITY OF SOUTHERN CALIFORNIA

The Latino Alumni Association has hosted many events to engage their alumni. They host a golf classic, scholarship dinner, and fundraisers. They also host a Q&A session with the chair of the alumni board.

UNIVERSITY OF WASHINGTON

The Multi-cultural Alumni Partnership works with the community, alumni, and students to promote scholarships and support for minorities. They also host the annual Distinguished Alumni and Community Award focused on bridging the gap in achievement.

The first step in adopting these model programs is to find out more about them. We suggest contacting the development and alumni relations staffs at these institutions. Through our interviews, we found that these individuals are a wealth of information, are excited and eager to share, and have worked out many of the kinks in starting new programs.

9

MISTAKES TO AVOID

Giving to education is a major thrust of giving among alumni of color. However, many colleges and universities do not reach out to them, assuming that they will not give, as noted throughout this book (Gasman & Bowman, 2011). Only more education on the part of development officers will dispel these myths about alumni of color and giving. There are several major problems with colleges and universities in terms of their relationships with alumni of color. We discuss these below.

NOT BEING ASKED

First, as mentioned, alumni of color are often not asked to give nor are they engaged in any substantial way by colleges (Gasman & Bowman, 2011).

FAILING TO SEE THE RETURN ON INVESTMENT

Second, many colleges and universities do not see a return on investment when it pertains to alumni of color (Gasman & Bowman, 2011). Development officers are not convinced that the work needed to engage alumni of color will pay off in terms of future giving. Many times these individuals (and their supervisors) want to see numbers in terms of the potential for giving among alumni of color and, until then, they are not convinced of the value of pursuing them. That said, it is impossible to gather data on alumni of color at the institutional level if colleges and universities do not reach out to alumni of color (Gasman & Bowman, 2011).

ASSUMING WAYS OF INVOLVEMENT WITHOUT ASKING

The third problem is that colleges and universities do not ask alumni of color how they would like to be engaged when they finally do reach out. Rather, they assume the ways that alumni of color want to be involved with the institution. It is important to ask alumni of color specifically how they would like to work with the institution as close and meaningful connections lead to greater engagement and increased giving (Gasman & Bowman, 2011).

FAILING TO INVOLVE ALUMNI OF COLOR IN LEADERSHIP ROLES

Fourth, colleges and universities rarely involve alumni of color in alumni leadership positions (Gasman & Bowman, 2011). This is particularly off-putting, as most alumni of color do not want to give to or engage with an organization that does not see them as a potential leader within the organization. From time to time we hear development officers say, "But we can't get the prominent alumni of color leaders to be on our boards." The problem with this statement is that colleges and universities need to be grooming leaders and asking a diverse group of alumni of color leaders to engage with their institutions. Too often, the same alumni of color leaders are tapped over and over while there are many other leaders with the potential to contribute (Gasman & Bowman, 2011). According to Gitin (2001), "Diverse leaders can expand knowledge, create new resources and open doors to partnerships necessary to fulfill an organization's mission" (p. 77). Board diversity is vital to strengthening and growing an organization (Siciliano, 1996). It results in reaching new constituents and potential donors, representing college and university alumni in more accurate ways, and a wider knowledge base (Gitin, 2001). Gitin offers an interesting approach to board diversification. She explains that most boards, including alumni boards, ask the question "Who are we missing?" when thinking about board diversity. Instead, they should be asking "How do we need to change [our organization] in order to attract those we want to recruit?" The problem is that often organizations do not want to change. However, change is necessary and unavoidable with the coming demographic diversity at colleges and universities. It is best to be out in front, leading the way and demonstrating the benefits and results of diversity.

LACK OF COMPENSATION FOR NEGATIVE EXPERIENCES

Fifth, most colleges and universities fail to realize that alumni of color have often had negative experiences while on campus and harbor negative feelings toward their alma mater as a result of these negative experiences (Gasman & Bowman, 2011). It is vital that these experiences be acknowledged and that alumni of color be brought up to date on the experiences of current alumni of color – which are hopefully vastly improved. If an alumnus is disgruntled, the best way to reengage them is to ask them to help with the very issue that may have made them angry or severed the ties with their alma mater. Addressing the problem shows the alumnus that the institution is serious about making change.

LEAVING ALUMNI OF COLOR OUT

Sixth, often alumni of color do not see themselves depicted in university publications. The majority of fundraising publications depict scenes of majority students and events that are important in the lives of White students, ignoring the events and experiences that resonate with alumni of color (Gasman & Bowman, 2011). For example, at Indiana University, fundraising brochures have long depicted Little 500, an historic bike race that takes place on the campus every year. When the bike race began, Black students were not included and as such created their own event – a Black Picnic in a meadow on campus. To this day, these events take place separately on the same day. However, only one of the events is celebrated by the institution and highlighted in publications.

Often fundraising brochures and direct mail solicitations include stereotypical pictures of alumni of color. Typically, the pictures are of older White males standing over some school children. Alumni of color want to see photos and depictions of themselves as central to the institution and do not want to be invisible or on the periphery. Institutional advancement professionals need to work with communications professionals to engage multiple audiences with their publications. In addition, it is important to have targeted publications that speak only and specifically to various alumni of color audiences. The secret to successful engagement is to include alumni of color in general publications and to provide them with a venue of their own (Gasman & Bowman, 2011).

LACK OF STAFF KNOWLEDGE

A final mistake is a lack of knowledge on the part of advancement staff. Although knowledge of alumni of color motivations for giving on the part of staff is important on minority-serving institution campuses, it is downright crucial on historically White campuses. The majority of White America knows little about people of color and the majority of advancement staffs are White. Unlike people of color, Whites are not forced to operate in a nation that is steeped in another race's cultural values. Thus, sometimes White advancement professionals do not understand cultural differences in giving; they do not understand what is important to communities of color affiliated with their institutions. For this reason, it is important that advancement staff find out as much information as they can – survey alumni, hold focus groups (and be willing to listen to what people have to say), read books and articles on philanthropy in communities of color and African American giving specifically. One very practical suggestion is to read materials as a staff and then have a conversation, design strategies, and make changes to the institution's approach (Gasman, 2002; Gasman & Bowman, 2011).

THE OVERALL CAMPUS EXPERIENCE AND ITS CONNECTION TO FUNDRAISING

Although most fundraising professionals do not consider themselves part of the inner workings of the lives of students on campus, they are nonetheless. In order for alumni of color to feel connected to campuses and engaged enough to give back to campus, it is imperative that they have positive experiences while on campus. Advancement Vice Presidents have the ear of the president and bring in financial resources that sustain the campus and as such they can play a substantial role in institutional change. Unless historically White campuses are more inclusive – beyond just recruiting students of color – alumni of color will not give. They want to see change. They want to see more people of color among students, administrators, and faculty. And, they want to see the accomplishments and efforts of people like them recognized on campus. Those in institutional advancement can play a part in making this kind of systemic change by being vocal about the changes that need to take place in order to garner alumni of color support (Gasman & Bowman, 2011).

10

BEST PRACTICES AND CONCLUDING THOUGHTS

As demonstrated throughout this book, there are common themes within communities of color and these themes can be instrumental in shaping fundraising approaches and strategies used by colleges and universities to engage and solicit them.

Among all communities of color, generational patterns, and level of assimilation matter in terms of fundraising. The longer a person has been in the United States, the more he or she will resemble the majority in terms of her philanthropy. Among some groups, assimilation takes place more rapidly as they want to be accepted by the mainstream United States. Considering generational status and the level of assimilation among your institutional alumni, which takes some background research, is directly related to fundraising success.

Related to this idea of assimilation is emergency giving. All racial and ethnic minorities begin their philanthropy by giving to their families, typically for emergencies. When alumni of color are less affluent and less assimilated, this emergency giving is quite common. However, as they become more assimilated, giving begins to take a turn and is typically focused on quality of life issues, including culture, health, education, and the arts. As alumni of color become more affluent, they give in more formal ways.

Majority institutions need to be respectful of the cultural traditions of their alumni of color. All too often, traditions other than those of the majority are ignored and overlooked – sometimes on purpose, sometimes out of ignorance. Development and alumni relations staff should familiarize themselves with the cultural traditions of their alumni and capitalize on these traditions. The best way to become familiar is to ask alumni of color to share their cultures with others during the academic year as well as during events like homecoming and alumni weekend. Everyone on campus will benefit from this sharing of perspectives.

When learning about other cultures in order to increase your institution's fundraising strength and capabilities, it is essential to remember that there are vast differences among alumni of color and within the various ethnic subcultures. Fundraisers should learn about these differences and design strategies and engagement that consider them.

Majority institutions also need to remember that immigration is an important issue to many racial and ethnic minorities, especially Latinos and Asians. People have different feelings about and perspectives on immigration and letting these thoughts, if they are negative, shape your fundraising approach is not advantageous. Latinos and Asians care about immigration issues and will support programs and research that speaks to these issues. Ignoring this fact only hinders your institution and keeps it at a distance from your alumni.

Colleges and universities are primed for philanthropic giving among racial and ethnic minorities more than any other entity apart from the church. All of these groups value education as a means of growing and enhancing their communities. They just need to know how your institution has aided in this process and what it will do in the future. Education is seen as a tool for both individual and collective forms of empowerment. Alumni of color want to become more self-sufficient and philanthropy is a mechanism for self-sufficiency and community prosperity. This is a very different perspective and approach from the White majority as, by and large, they have not had to use education for collective empowerment, only individual advancement.

It is vital to remember that for most racial and ethnic minorities, community is more important than the individual. Alumni of color are interested in learning about your institution's commitment to uplifting the next generation and how you are making the experiences of students of color more meaningful. They see individual success as part of and representative of community success. Talking to this belief instead of merely emphasizing individual achievements and the American dream is advantageous.

Another factor to remember when engaging and soliciting alumni of color is that enlisting the support of well-respected individuals in the particular racial or ethnic minority's community can be beneficial if not essential. Alumni of color want to be engaged by people who look like them. It makes them feel comfortable, respected and listened to in the fundraising process.

Development officers need to be aware of the issue of trust and how it manifests in giving. Throughout this book, we have mentioned how important trust is and how it shapes the giving habits of the various racial and ethnic minorities. One of the most important manifestations of this lack of trust is that most people of color avoid "pass through" organizations when giving – these are the more organized and formal mechanisms for giving in society, such as the Salvation Army or United Way.

Keeping fundraising less formal and more personal is vital with alumni of color.

Another issue to keep in mind when engaging alumni of color is their respect for their elders, especially among Latinos, AAPIs, and Native Americans. Programs and research that speak to the needs and issues of the elderly are likely to be supported by alumni of color.

One of the most important factors related to giving among alumni of color is the way they are overlooked. As we have said, all too often the White majority sees racial and ethnic minorities as receivers of philanthropy rather than potential givers. College and university advancement and alumni relations staff must change this mindset immediately and see their alumni of color as donors. Although much of philanthropy in communities of color goes unseen, many donors now want to be heard and seen rather than giving in silence. They want their communities to get credit for the giving that has taken place for centuries. This fact, combined with the growing demographics on college campuses, makes this an opportune time to tap into the potential of alumni of color.

The last factor to keep in mind when approaching alumni of color is that they want to see concrete results from their giving. This need cuts across all racial and ethnic minorities and is connected to issues of trust. Although the need for concrete results can be frustrating to fundraisers at majority institutions, with time, alumni of color will learn to give without seeing immediate and concrete results. Once trust is established they are much more likely to give to endowments, which are often a very foreign concept to people of color. An investment of time will yield positive results.

In order for colleges and universities, as well as the fundraising profession, to move forward in their efforts to engage and solicit alumni of color, they need to consider this endeavor important, direct budgetary support toward these efforts, and spend time acquiring a basic knowledge about the various cultures that are now prominent in the United States. Not only is this the right thing to do but, it is essential to the bottom line of any institution of higher education.

College and university advancement and alumni staff members need to move away from traditional ideas about philanthropy and fundraising, opening their minds to new ideas and admitting that this is a lot to learn in this ever changing world. Instead of being fearful of saying the wrong thing, colleges and universities need to take a chance and engage their alumni of color.

As mentioned throughout the book, the majority of development and alumni relations staff members are White in the United States despite the fact that the student and alumni demographics are changing rapidly and have been changing over the last 20 years significantly. The most significant change that majority institutions can make is to begin to diversify their fundraising staff. According to Wagner and Ryan (2004), "It is interesting and, indeed, slightly alarming that minorities are still very underrepresented [in the fundraising profession] and that the most influential professional societies of fundraising practitioners are not actively addressing the issue, especially at a time when an increasingly diverse American population is looking outward to ways of sharing their diverse values" (p. 64). Majority institutions need to stop making excuses – "We can't find fundraisers of color" – and be creative in their recruitment. Fundraisers of color can be garnered from other areas of the college or university and trained to be fundraisers. They can also be culled from business, especially sales, and retrained in the area of fundraising. Lastly, colleges and universities can grow their own fundraisers by tapping students with fundraising potential. Students (future alumni) are not only ambassadors of the institution, but they have a sense of commitment and loyalty to the institution that can be harnessed in ways that bolsters their fundraising ability. These future alumni can also speak directly to the quality of both the academic and co-curricular programs. They know the faculty members, the coaches, those working in the residence halls. And the special services on campus that speak to the needs of students of color. Working with students of color to train them to be future fundraisers is one of the very best ways to cultivate fundraisers of color. Yes, this takes time and energy, but what is the alternative? Institutions that do not diversify their fundraising enterprises will be left behind in terms of fundraising success in the future as the landscape as well as the major players are changing. Will you be ready?

11

STRATEGIES AT A GLANCE

Racial or Ethnic Group	Strategy
African Americans	Tie engagement or solicitation to the notion of racial uplift
African Americans, Latinos	Tie engagement and solicitation to scholarships
African Americans, Latinos (less affluent)	Concentrate on concrete causes and tie giving opportunity to issues with visible results
African Americans, Latinos, Asian Americans & Pacific Islanders	Focus on civil rights issues and how your institution is addressing them through research and practice
African Americans, Native Americans	Focus on health related issues that impact the community and how your institution is addressing them through research and practice
African Americans, Latinos, Asian American & Pacific Islanders, and Native Americans (less affluent)	Start small when soliciting them and gradually work toward larger gifts that are connected with community values

Racial or Ethnic Group	Strategy
African Americans, Latinos, Asian American & Pacific Islanders, and Native Americans	Spend time establishing trust through engagement efforts before soliciting them
African Americans, Latinos, Asian American & Pacific Islanders, and Native Americans	Make giving opportunities familial in nature
African Americans, Latinos, Asian American & Pacific Islanders, and Native Americans	Respect the culture of the prospective donor
African Americans	Capitalize on group membership and set up giving circles in conjunction with this membership
Latinos, Asian Americans & Pacific Islanders	Spend time explaining how philanthropy contributes to the nation, community, and institution
Asian Americans & Pacific Islanders	Avoid aggressive fundraising; be subtle
Latinos, Asian Americans & Pacific Islanders, Native Americans	Show immense respect for the elders in the potential donor's community
Native Americans	Don't assume that the donor wants public recognition. Always ask.
Latinos, Asian Americans & Pacific Islanders (more affluent)	Solicit for a gift after the potential donor has been involved in the institution, preferably serving in a leadership role
African Americans, Latinos, Asian American & Pacific Islanders, and Native Americans	Tie engagement and gift solicitation to the issue of education, demonstrating the ways your institution is enhancing educational opportunities
Latinos, Asian American & Pacific Islanders, and Native Americans	Tie engagement and gift solicitations to institutional research and practice that focuses on the elderly in the specific community

Racial or Ethnic Group	Strategy
Latinos, Asian American & Pacific Islanders, and Native Americans	Consider enlisting the advice and assistance of a respected individual in the specific community when approaching a potential donor
African Americans, Latinos, Asian American & Pacific Islanders, and Native Americans	Demonstrate your institution's role in enhancing the local communities in which the potential donor lives or from which she hails
Latinos	Demonstrate ways that your institution is working on issues related to immigration, either research or practice
African Americans, Latinos, Asian American & Pacific Islanders, and Native Americans	Consider members of these groups for volunteer leadership roles in your alumni relations effort as well as your campaign efforts
African Americans, Latinos, Asian American & Pacific Islanders, and Native Americans	Make an effort to educate yourself and your staff on the giving habits and cultural traditions of each of these groups – not just once but continually
Latinos	Demonstrate the way your college or university is working to eradicate poverty in your community and elsewhere through research and practice
Latinos	Make connections for alumni to arts and culture activities related to Latinos on your campus
African Americans, Latinos, Asian American & Pacific Islanders, and Native Americans	Tie engagement and solicitation efforts to local youth programs and community education. Demonstrate how your institution works with local nonprofits and schools to provide programs for youth.
African Americans, Latinos, Asian American & Pacific Islanders, and Native Americans	Don't assume that any of these groups understand philanthropy the way that mainstream individuals do
African Americans, Latinos, Asian American & Pacific Islanders, and Native Americans	Don't look upon any of these groups are ONLY recipients of philanthropy. Instead consider them potential philanthropists and donors.

Racial or Ethnic Group	Strategy
Native Americans	Emphasize connections between giving and self-sufficiency, demonstrating the way your institution can enable self-sufficiency among tribal communities
Native Americans	Tie engagement and giving to community uplift within tribal communities
Asian Americans & Pacific Islanders (more affluent)	Tie engagement and giving to the issue of prestige
Native Americans	Don't make ties to prestige or rank or individualism. Emphasize community over the individual.
Native Americans	Tie engagement and giving to cultural preservation efforts with which your college or university is involved
African Americans, Latinos, Asian American & Pacific Islanders, and Native Americans	Consider having a development officer of the same race or, at the very least, another person of color solicit these donors
African Americans, Latinos, Asian American & Pacific Islanders, and Native Americans	Include stories about these groups in alumni magazines and on websites
African Americans, Latinos, Asian American & Pacific Islanders, and Native Americans	Demonstrate how your college or university is committed to diversity, using qualitative and quantitative data
African Americans, Latinos, Asian American & Pacific Islanders, and Native Americans	If a racial incident occurs, explain it to the group affected

APPENDICES

APPENDIX A

American Association of Universities (all surveyed for this study)

Brandeis University
Brown University
California Institute of Technology
Carnegie Mellon University
Case Western Reserve University
Columbia University
Cornell University
Duke University
Emory University
Georgia Institute of Technology
Harvard University
Indiana University
Iowa State University
The Johns Hopkins University
Massachusetts Institute of Technology
McGill University
Michigan State University

New York University
Northwestern University
The Ohio State University
The Pennsylvania State University
Princeton University
Purdue University
Rice University
Rutgers, The State University of New Jersey
Stanford University
Stony Brook University-State University of New York
Texas A&M University
Tulane University
The University of Arizona
University at Buffalo, The State University of New York
University of California, Berkeley
University of California, Davis
University of California, Irvine
University of California, Los Angeles
University of California, San Diego
University of California, Santa Barbara
The University of Chicago
University of Colorado at Boulder
University of Florida
University of Illinois at Urbana-Champaign
The University of Iowa
The University of Kansas
University of Maryland, College Park
University of Michigan
University of Minnesota
University of Missouri-Columbia
The University of North Carolina, Chapel Hill
University of Oregon
University of Pennsylvania
University of Pittsburgh

University of Rochester
University of Southern California
The University of Texas at Austin
University of Toronto
University of Virginia
University of Washington
The University of Wisconsin-Madison
Vanderbilt University
Washington University in St. Louis
Yale University

APPENDIX B

Institutions Interviewed for Study

Brown University
Columbia University
Cornell University
Emory University
New York University
The Ohio State University
Pennsylvania State University
Rutgers University
Texas A&M University
University of Arizona
University of California, Berkeley
University of California, Los Angeles (UCLA)
University of North Carolina, Chapel Hill
University of Southern California
University of Virginia
University of Washington
Vanderbilt University
Yale University

APPENDIX C

Essential Guide to Alumni of Color: Interview Questions

Student Initiative Questions

1. What is the current ethnic makeup of your student body?
2. Are there initiatives in place to attract a more diverse student body?
   a. Is there specific funding set-aside?
3. Once on campus, what diversity initiatives are in place for students of color to align with?
4. How are these various initiatives decided on?
   a. Are they student, faculty, or administration driven?
5. How are students encouraged to get involved? Give specific examples.
   a. Describe your most successful method.
6. Are faculty and staff trained or counseled on interacting with different cultures?
7. Does the institution have defined outcomes for these initiatives?
   a. How are these outcomes measured?
8. Is there a central body or department that sets policy and coordinates diversity programs?

Alumni Engagement Questions

1. What alumni staff positions support your work targeting alumni of color?
2. Do you target each of the student affinity groups referred to above as alumni groups?
3. What percent of your alumni are represented by people of color [e.g. African Heritage, Hispanic, Asian and Pacific Islander, other]?
   a. How do you track this?

4. What initiatives are in place to reach and engage alumni communities of color?
5. What are the current levels of giving from alumni communities of color?
   a. How do you track this?
   b. How do these compare to overall alumni numbers?

Communication

1. What types of alumni outreach/communication tools do you currently use?
   a. Which are most successful? Why?
2. Who/what team/what department writes designs and produces your general alumni materials?
3. Who/what team/what department writes designs and produces your ethnic-specific alumni materials?
4. Please describe your efforts in helping graduating students make the transition into alumni. What cultivation activities do you have prior to graduation?

Miscellaneous Information

1. In the last 15 years, have there been any racial incidents on your campus? Briefly describe.
2. Are there any current or lingering racial tensions on your campus? Briefly describe.
3. How do you describe current race relations on your campus?

APPENDIX D

Alumni of Color Survey (distributed to AAU member institutions)

1. Does your institution have alumni of color association(s)? If so, are there different associations for different racial/ethnic groups?

2. Are there race/ethnic group specific events at class reunions?
   YES
   NO
3. Do alumni of color attend reunions in the same ratios as their White counterparts?
   YES
   NO
4. On average, what percentage of your student/alumni population is made up of people of color?
5. What percentage of your institution's donations come from alumni of color?
6. Does your institution have a Minority Alumni Affairs office? If so, how large is the staff?
7. How many people of color work within development or fundraising at your institution? What percentage is this of the total amount of people who work at these offices?
8. Is there a distinction between the publications or emails sent out to the general alumni population and the alumni of color population?
   YES
   NO
9. What percentage of your alumni of color were international students during their undergraduate career?
10. Which age group of alumni of color historically donates the greatest amount to the institution?
11. Which age group of alumni of color historically donates the greatest amount to the institution?
    0–10 years since graduation
    11–20 years since graduation
    21–30 years since graduation
    31–40 years since graduation
    41–50 years since graduation
    50+ years since graduation

APPENDIX E

Alumni of Color Alumni Survey

1. Undergraduate Institution:
2. Graduate Institution:
3. Year of Graduation:
4. Race/Ethnicity:
5. Do you give to your alma mater? If yes, why do you give?
6. If you do not give, why don't you give?
7. Do you volunteer with your alma mater? If yes, why, and in what ways?
8. If you do not volunteer, why don't you?
9. How would you like your alma mater to engage you?
10. How would you like your alma mater to solicit you?
11. General comments

BIBLIOGRAPHY

Aguilar, O., Duenas, T., Glores, B., Godinez, L., Joy, H., & Zavala, I. (November 2005). *Fairness in philanthropy part I: Foundation giving to minority-led nonprofits*. Retrieved from The Greenlining Institute website: www.philanthropy.iupui.edu/Millennium/usefulInformation/Fairness%20in%20Philanthropy.pdf.

Ahuja, S., Gupta, P., & Petsod, D. (2004). *Arab, Middle Eastern, Muslim, and South Asian communities in the San Francisco Bay area*. Retrieved from Grantmakers Concerned with Immigrants and Refugees and Asian Americans/Pacific Islanders in Philanthropy website: www.sff.org/about/publications/documents-publications/AME_report.pdf.

Aluli-Meyer, M. (2008). Indigenous and authentic: Native Hawaiian epistemology and the triangulation of meaning. In L. Smith, N. Denzin, & Y. Lincoln (eds.), *Handbook of critical and indigenous methodologies*, pp. 217–32. Thousand Oaks, CA: Sage.

Anft, M. (October 18, 2001). Raising money with sense and sensibility. *The Chronicle of Philanthropy*. Retrieved from: http://philanthropy.com/article/Raising-Money-With-Sense-and/52257/.

Anft, M. (January 10, 2002). Tapping ethnic wealth. *The Chronicle of Philanthropy*. Retrieved from: http://philanthropy.com/article/Tapping-Ethnic-Wealth/51923/.

Anand, P. (2003). Hindu diaspora and religious philanthropy in the United States. Paper given at the 6th International Society for Third Sector Research, Toronto.

Anderson, J. A. (1988). *The education of Blacks in the South, 1865–1930.* Chapel Hill, NC: University of North Carolina Press.

ASHE (2011). ASHE Higher Education Report. *Special Issue: Philanthropy and Fundraising in American Higher Education*, 37(2), 1–155. doi: 10.1002/aehe.3702.

Asian American/Pacific Islander Philanthropy (2001). *AAPIP traditions 2001 annual report.* Retrieved from Asian American/Pacific Islander Philanthropy website: www.aapip.org/images/stories/publications/annualreport/doc/AAPIP-AnnualReport-2001.pdf.

Asian American/Pacific Islander Philanthropy (2002). *AAPIP building bridges 2002 annual report.* Retrieved from Asian American/Pacific Islander Philanthropy website: www.aapip.org/images/stories/publications/annualreport/doc/AAPIP-AnnualReport-2002.pdf.

Asian American/Pacific Islander Philanthropy (2002). *Flash bulletin fall 2002* [Bulletin]. Retrieved from: www.aapip.org/images/stories/publications/flash/doc/flash%20fall%202002%20.pdf.

Asian American/Pacific Islander Philanthropy (2003). *Flash bulletin fall 2003* [Bulletin]. Retrieved from: www.aapip.org/images/stories/publications/flash/doc/flash%20fall%202003.pdf.

Asian American/Pacific Islander Philanthropy (2003). *AAPIP . . . between philanthropy and our communities 2003 annual report.* Retrieved from Asian American/Pacific Islander Philanthropy website: www.aapip.org/images/stories/publications/annualreport/doc/AAPIP-AnnualReport-2003.pdf.

Asian American/Pacific Islander Philanthropy (2003). *New challenges for bay area philanthropy: Asian & Pacific Islander communities.* Retrieved from Asian American/Pacific Islander Philanthropy website: www.aapip.org/images/stories/publications/research/doc/AAPIP%20Census.pdf.

Asian American/Pacific Islander Philanthropy (2004). *Flash bulletin fall 2004* [Bulletin]. Retrieved from: www.aapip.org/images/stories/publications/flash/doc/flash%20fall%202004.pdf.

Asian American/Pacific Islander Philanthropy (2005). *2005 annual report AAPIP.* Retrieved from Asian American/Pacific Islander Philanthropy website: www.aapip.org/images/stories/publications/annualreport/doc/AAPIP-AnnualReport-2005.pdf.

Asian American/Pacific Islander Philanthropy (spring 2005). *Flash bulletin spring 2005* [Bulletin]. Retrieved from: www.aapip.org/images/stories/publications/flash/doc/flash%20spring%202005.pdf.

Asian American/Pacific Islander Philanthropy (winter 2005). *Flash bulletin winter 2005* [Bulletin]. Retrieved from: www.aapip.org/images/stories/publications/flash/doc/flash%20winter%202005.pdf.

Asian American/Pacific Islander Philanthropy (2005). *Flash bulletin 2005 end of the year* [Bulletin]. Retrieved from: www.aapip.org/images/stories/publications/flash/doc/flash%20year%20end%202005.pdf.

Asian American/Pacific Islander Philanthropy (2006). *2006 annual report.* Retrieved from Asian American/Pacific Islander Philanthropy website: www.aapip.org/images/stories/publications/annualreport/doc/AAPIP-AnnualReport-2006.pdf.

Asian American/Pacific Islander Philanthropy (2006). *Giving to Asian Pacific American communities.* Retrieved from Asian American/Pacific Islander Philanthropy website: www.aapip.org/images/stories/publications/research/doc/Fact%20Sheet%20-%20Giving%20to%20APAs.pdf.

Asian American/Pacific Islander Philanthropy (summer 2006). *Flash bulletin summer 2006* [Bulletin]. Retrieved from: www.aapip.org/images/stories/publications/flash/doc/flash%20summer%202006.pdf.

Asian American/Pacific Islander Philanthropy (winter 2006). *Flash bulletin winter 2006* [Bulletin]. Retrieved from: www.aapip.org/images/stories/publications/flash/doc/flash%20winter%202005.pdf.

Asian American/Pacific Islander Philanthropy (2007). *2007 annual report.* Retrieved from Asian American/Pacific Islander Philanthropy website: www.aapip.org/images/stories/publications/research/doc/AAPIP-GOpps4WWW.pdf.

Asian American/Pacific Islander Philanthropy (summer 2007). *Flash bulletin summer 2007* [Bulletin]. Retrieved from: www.aapip.org/images/stories/publications/flash/doc/flash%20summer%202007.pdf.

Asian American/Pacific Islander Philanthropy (winter 2007). *Flash bulletin winter 2007* [Bulletin]. Retrieved from: www.aapip.org/images/stories/publications/flash/doc/flash%20winter%202007.pdf.

Asian American/Pacific Islander Philanthropy (2008). *2008 annual report.* Retrieved from Asian American/Pacific Islander Philanthropy website: www.aapip.org/images/stories/publications/annualreport/doc/AAPIP-AnnualReport-2008.pdf

Asian American/Pacific Islander Philanthropy (2008). *Flash bulletin fall 2008* [Bulletin]. Retrieved from: www.aapip.org/images/stories/publications/flash/doc/flash%20fall%202008.pdf.

Asian American/Pacific Islander Philanthropy (2009). *Flash bulletin winter 2009* [Bulletin]. Retrieved from: www.aapip.org/images/stories/publications/flash/doc/flash%20winter%202009.pdf.

Asian American/Pacific Islander Philanthropy (2010). *Giving back, giving together: Starting a giving circle in your community* [Brochure]. Retrieved from: www.aapip.org/images/stories/programs/cp/doc/giving_circle_brochure.pdf.

Asian American Giving. (2009). *Fast facts: Charitable giving.* Retrieved from: www.asianamericangiving.com/fast-facts-charitable-giv.html.

Asian American giving—the Chinese connection: A new force is emerging in the philanthropic world (December 9, 2002). Committee of 100. Retrieved from: www.committee100.org/media/media_eng/120902/html.

Bartolini, W. F. (2001). Using a communication perspective to manage diversity in the development office. *New Directions for Philanthropic Fundraising, 34,* 47–76. doi: 10.1002/pf.3403.

Bearman, J., Ramos, H. A. J., & Pond, A. N. S. (2010). Moving diversity up the agenda: Lessons and next steps from the diversity in philanthropy project. *The Foundation Review, 2,* 85–99. Retrieved from: http://dx.doi.org/10.4087/FOUNDATIONREVIEW-D-10-00005.

Berry, M. L. (n.d.). Native-American philanthropy: Expanding social participation and self-determination. Retrieved from: www.cof.org/files/documents/publications/cultures_of_caring/nativeamerican.pdf.

Blau, J. R. & Heying, C. (1996). Historically black organizations in the nonprofit sector: A reply to Atlanta metro y. *Nonprofit and Voluntary Sector Quarterly, 25*(4), 540–2. Retrieved from: www.mackcenter.org/swj_db/articles/140.

Brown, K. (2012). *Diversity in philanthropy.* Retrieved from Diversity in Philanthropy website: www.diversityinphilanthropy.org/.

Burbridge, L. C. (n.d.). *Diversity in foundations: The numbers and their meaning.* Retrieved from: www.philanthropy.iupui.edu/Millennium/usefulInformation/Diversity%20in%20Foundations%20(Numbers%20&%20Meaning%20).pdf.

Burbridge, L. C. (1995). *Status of African Americans in grantmaking institutions.* Indianapolis, IN: Center on Philanthropy at Indiana University.

Burlingame, D. F. & Hulse, L. (1991). *Taking fund raising seriously: Advancing the profession and practice of raising money.* San Francisco, CA: Jossey-Bass.

Butler, J. S. (2005). *Entrepreneurship and self-help among black Americans.* Albany, NY: SUNY Press.

Campoamor, D., Diaz, W. A., & Ramos, H. A. J. (1999). *Nuevos senderos: Reflections on Hispanics and philanthropy.* Houston, TX: Arte Publico Press.

Capek, M. E. S. & Mead, M. (2006). *Effective philanthropy: Organizational success through deep diversity and gender equality.* Cambridge, MA: MIT Press.

Carson, E. D. (1987). The charitable activities of black Americans: A portrait of self-help? *The Review of Black Political Economy, 15*(3), 100–11. doi: 10.1007/BF02903995.

Carson, E. D. (1989). *The charitable appeals fact book: How black and white Americans respond to different types of fund-raising efforts.* Washington, DC and Lanham, MD: Joint Center for Political Studies Press.

Carson, E. (1993a). *A hand up: African American philanthropy and self-help in America.* New York: University Press of America.

Carson, E. D. (1993b). The National Black United Fund: From movement for social change to social change organization. *New Directions for Philanthropic Fundraising,* 1, 53–71. doi: 10.1002/pf.41219930107.

Carson, E. D. (1993c). On race, gender, culture, and research on the voluntary sector. *Nonprofit Management and Leadership,* 3(3), 327–35. doi: 10.1002/nml.4130030311.

Carson, E. D. (1994). Community foundations, racial diversity, and institutional change. *New Directions for Philanthropic Fundraising,* 5, 33–43. doi: 10.1002/pf.41219940505.

Carson, E. D. (1994). Diversity and equity among foundation grantmakers. *Nonprofit Management and Leadership,* 3, 331–44. doi: 10.1002/nml.4130040307.

Carson, E. D. (1995). Understanding cultural difference in fundraising. *New Directions for Philanthropic Fundraising,* 10, 99–112. doi: 10.1002/pf.41219951010.

Carson, E. D. (1999). The role of indigenous and institutional philanthropy in advancing social justice. In C. T. Clofelter & T. Ehrlich (eds.), *Philanthropy and the nonprofit sector in a changing America,* pp. 249–74. Bloomington, IN: Indiana University Press.

Census Bureau. www.census.gov

Chafe, W. (1981). *Civilities and civil rights: Greensboro, North Carolina and the Black struggle for freedom.* New York: Oxford University Press.

Chaffin, L. (n.d.). *Philanthropy and the black church.* Retrieved from the Learning to Give website: http://learningtogive.org/papers/paper 47.html.

Chang, P., Williams, D., Griffith, E., & Young, J. (1994). Church-agency relationships in the Black community. *Nonprofit and Voluntary Sector Quarterly,* 23, 91-105.

Chao, J. (1999). Asian-American philanthropy: Expanding circles of participation. *Culture of caring.* Michigan: W. K. Kellogg Foundation. The Coalition for New Philanthropy (2004). *New York: Case study of the first three years: 2011–2003.* Retrieved from the Coalition for New Philanthropy website: www.philanthropy.iupui.edu/Millennium/usefulInformation/Coalition%20for%20New%20Philanthropy%20Case_Study.pdf.

Commission on Research on Asian American and Pacific Islander Research in Education (2011).

Conley, D. (2008). *Being black, living in the red: Race, wealth, and social policy in America*. Berkeley, CA: University of California Press.

Copeland-Carson, J. (2005). Promoting diversity in contemporary Black philanthropy: Toward a new conceptual model. *New Directions for Philanthropic Fundraising, 48*, 77–88.

Cortés, M. (1995). Three strategic questions about Latino philanthropy. *New Directions for Philanthropic Fundraising, 8*, 23–40. doi: 10.1002/pf.41219950804.

Cortés, M. (1999). Do Hispanic nonprofits foster Hispanic philanthropy? *Philanthropic Fundraising, 1999*, 31–40.

Cortés, M. (2002). Questions about Hispanics and fundraising. *Fundraising in Diverse Cultural Environments, 37*, 45–54. doi: 10.1002/pf.5.

Davis, K. E. (1975). *Fund raising in the black community: History, feasibility, and conflict*. Lanham, MD: Scarecrow Press.

Dewey, B. I. (2006). Fundraising for large public university libraries: Margins for excellence. *Library Leadership and Management, 20*(1), 5–12. Retrieved from: http://llama.metapress.com/content/h4315j51p4768511//.

Diversity in Philanthropy (2012). Diversity in philanthropy. Retrieved from D5 website: www.diversityinphilanthropy.org/.

Duckett, M. (September 28, 2011). Author's Spotlight: Q&A with Valaida Fullwood.

Duran, L. (2001). Caring for each other: Philanthropy in communities of color. *Grassroots Fundraising Journal*, 4–7.

Edmunds, R. D. (1995). Native Americans, new voices: American Indian history, 1895–1995. *The American Historical Review, 100*(3), 717–14. Retrieved from: www.jstor.org/stable/2168602.

Edmondson, V. & Carroll, A. (1999). Giving back: An examination of the philanthropic motivations, orientations and activities of large Black-Owned Businesses. *Journal of Business Ethics, 19*, 171–9.

Ford Foundation (2003). *Latino philanthropy: Literature review*. New York: Center on Philanthropy and Civil Society.

Formative Evaluation Research Associates (FERA) (2002). *Engaging communities of color*. Retrieved from: ww2.wkkf.org/DesktopModules/WKF.00_DmaSupport/ViewDoc.aspx?fld=PDFFile&CID=0&ListID=28&ItemID=23779&LanguageID=0.

Foundation Center (2011). *Foundation funding for Hispanics/Latinos in the United States and for Latin America*. Washington, DC: Foundation Center.

Fullwood, V. (2011). *Giving back: A tribute to generations of African American philanthropy*. New York: John F. Blair Publications.

Fulton, K., Kasper, G., & Kibbe, B. (July 2010). *What's next for philanthropy: Acting bigger and adapting better in a networked world*. Retrieved from the

Monitor Institute website: http://monitorinstitute.com/downloads/ Whats_Next_for_Philanthropy.pdf.

Gallegos, H. E. (1991). *Hispanics and the nonprofit sector*, ed. M. O'Neill. New York: Foundation Center.

Garrow, D. (1987). *Philanthropy and the Civil Rights Movement*. New York: Center for the Study of Philanthropy.

Gasman, M. (2002). An untapped resource: Bringing African Americans into the college and university giving process. *The CASE International Journal of Educational Advancement*, 2(3), 13–20.

Gasman, M. (2005). Sisters in service: African American sororities and the philanthropic support of education. In A. Walton (ed.), *Women, philanthropy, and education*, pp. 194–214. Bloomington, IN: Indiana University Press.

Gasman, M. (2007). *Envisioning Black colleges: A history of the United Negro College Fund*. Baltimore, MD: Johns Hopkins University Press.

Gasman, M. (2010). A growing tradition? Examining the African American family foundation. *Nonprofit Management & Leadership*, 21(2), 23–41.

Gasman, M. (2011a). Passive activism? African American fraternities and sororities and their role in the Civil Rights Movement. In M. W. Hughley & G. S. Parks (eds.), *Empirical studies of Black Greek letter organizations*, pp. 128–47. Oxford, MS: University of Mississippi Press.

Gasman, M. (2011b). Perceptions of Black college presidents: Sorting through stereotypes and reality to gain a complex picture. *American Education Research Journal*, 48(4), 836–70.

Gasman, M. & Anderson-Thompkins, S. (2003). *Fundraising from Black College alumni: Successful strategies for supporting alma mater*. Washington, DC: Council for the Advancement and Support of Education.

Gasman, M. & Bowman, N. (2011). Cultivating and soliciting donors of color. *Advancing Philanthropy*, 23–8.

Gasman, M. & Drezner, N. (2009). A maverick in the field: The Oram Group and fundraising in the Black College community during the 1970s. *History of Education Quarterly*, 49(4), 465–506.

Gasman, M. & Drezner, N. (2010). Fundraising for Black Colleges during the 1960s and 1970s: The case of Hampton Institute. *Nonprofit and Voluntary Sector Quarterly*, 39, 321–4.

Gasman, M. & Sedgwick, K. V. (eds) (2005). *Uplifting a people: Essays on African American philanthropy and education*. New York: Peter Lang.

Gasman, M., Baez, B., & Turner, C. (2007). *Understanding minority serving institutions*. Albany, NY: State University of New York Press.

Gasman, M., Louison, P., & Barnes, M. (2008). Giving and getting: A history of philanthropic activity among African American fraternities and sororities. In T. Brown, G. Parks, & C. Phillips (eds.), *Black Greek letter organizations in the Twentieth Century: Our fight has just begun*, pp. 203–31. Louisville, KY: University of Kentucky.

Gatewood Jr., W. B. (2000). *Aristocrats of color: The black elite, 1880–1920 (black community studies)*. Fayetteville, AR: The University of Arkansas Press.

Giddings, P. (2007). *In search of sisterhood: Delta Sigma Theta and the challenge of the Black sorority movement*. New York: William Morrow Publishers.

Gitin, M. (2001). Beyond representation: Building diverse board leadership teams. *New Directions for Philanthropic Fundraising*, 34, 77–100.

Give2Asia (2010). *Korean American philanthropy: Traditions, trends, and potential*. California: Give2Asia.

Give2Asia (2012). Asian philanthropy advisory network. Retrieved from: http://asianphilanthropy.org/.

Gonzales, L. (2010). *Increasing Latino engagement in sustainability and philanthropic efforts of mainstream youth development organizations in the United States* (Thesis). Retrieved from: http://via.library.depaul.edu/etd/30.

Gough Jr., S. N. (2001). Five reasons for nonprofit organizations to be inclusive. *New Directions for Philanthropic Fundraising*, 34, 101–18. doi: 10.1002/pf.3405.

Gupta, P. & Ritoper, S. (2007). *Growing opportunities: Will funding follow the rise in foundation assets and growth of AAPI populations?* Retrieved from Asian American/Pacific Islander Philanthropy website: www.aapip.org/images/stories/publications/annualreport/doc/AAPIP-AnnualReport-2007.pdf.

Hall-Russell, C. & Kasberg, R. (1997). *African American traditions of giving and serving: A Midwest perspective*. Indianapolis, IN: Center on Philanthropy at Indiana University.

Hamilton, C. H. & Lichman, W. R. (1995). *Cultures of giving II: How heritage, gender, wealth, and values influence philanthropy: New directions for philanthropic fundraising, no. 8*. Hoboken, NJ: Jossey-Bass.

Harmer, A. & Cotterrell, L. (September 2005). *Diversity in donorship: The changing landscape of official humanitarian aid*. Retrieved from the Humanitarian Policy Group website: www.odi.org.uk/resources/docs/275.pdf.

Hendricks, M. (1998). Why diversity matters. *New Directions for Philanthropic Fundraising*, 19, 115–26.

Herman, R. D. (2005). *The Jossey-Bass handbook of nonprofit leadership and management*. San Francisco, CA: Jossey-Bass.

Hine, D. C. (1997). *Hine sight: Black women and the re-construction of American history (blacks in the Diaspora)*. Bloomington, IN: Indiana University Press.

Ho, A. T. (November 2004). Asian-American philanthropy: Expanding knowledge, increasing possibilities (Working Papers No. 4). Retrieved from Georgetown University, The Center for Public & Nonprofit Leadership website: http://cpnl.georgetown.edu/doc_pool/WP04Ho.pdf.

Ho, A. T. (November 2008). *Asian American giving circles: Building bridges between philanthropy and our communities.* 37th Association for Research on Nonprofit Organization and Voluntary Action (ARNOVA) Conference, Philadelphia, PA.

Hoang, A. (June 1, 2011). *Understanding the giving preferences of the Chinese American Diaspora*. Retrieved from Give2Asia website: http://give2asia.org/?p=8647.

Holley, L. (2003). Emerging ethnic agencies: Building capacity to build community. *Journal of Community Practice,* 11(4), 39–57.

Holloman, D., Gasman, M., & Anderson-Thompkins, S. (2003). Motivations for philanthropic giving in the African American church: Implications for Black college fundraising. *Journal of Research on Christian Education,* 12(2), 137–69.

Hunt, E. (n.d.). *African American philanthropy: A legacy of giving*. Retrieved from the Twenty-First Century Foundation website: www.21cf.org/pdf/LegacyOfGiving.pdf.

Indiana University Center on Philanthropy (2010). *Giving USA*. Indianapolis, IN: Indiana University Center on Philanthropy.

Investing in a diverse democracy: Foundation giving to minority-led nonprofits (2006). Retrieved from the Greenlining Institute website: www.philanthropy.iupui.edu/Millennium/usefulInformation/Investing%20in%20a%20Diverse%20Democracy%20Foundation%20Giving%20to%20Minority%20Led%20Nonprofits.pdf.

IPEDS, National Center for Educational Statistics, Washington, D.C.

Jacobs, C. (1988). Benevolent societies of New Orleans during the late nineteenth and early twentieth century. *Louisiana History: The Journal of the Louisiana Historical Association,* 29(1), 21–33.

Johnson, R. E. (May 1989). Bill and Camille Cosby: First family of philanthropy. *Ebony,* 44(7), 25–34.

Kasper, G., Ramos, H. A., & Walker, C. (2004). Making the case for diversity in philanthropy. *Foundation News and Commentary,* 45(6), 17–23.

Kessel, F. (1989). Black foundations: Meeting vital needs. *Crisis,* 96(10), 14–18. Retrieved from ERIC database. (EJ415936).

Kim, B. S. & Johnson, A. S. (2011). Korean American philanthropy— traditions, trend, and potential. Retrieved from Give2Asia website:

http://give2asia.org/documents/Give2ASia-2011KoreanAmerican-Report.pdf.

Klein, K. (1998). Building a fundraising base that reflects the cultural diversity of the organization. *New Directions for Philanthropic Fundraising*, 20, 67–78.

Klein, K. (2007). *Fundraising for social change*. San Francisco, CA: Jossey-Bass.

Kumar, G. (ed.). (2003). *Indian Diaspora and giving patterns of Indian Americans in USA*. New Delhi, India: Charities Aid Foundation India.

Latino philanthropy literature review (2003). Retrieved from The City University of New York, The Graduate Center, Center on Philanthropy and Civil Society: www.philanthropy.org/programs/literature_reviews/latino_lit_review.pd.

Lee, R. (1990). *Guide to Chinese American philanthropy and charitable giving patterns*. San Rafael, CA: Pathway Press.

Lincoln, C. E. & Mamiya, L. H. (1990). *The Black church in the African American experience*. Raleigh, NC: Duke University Press.

Marga Incorporated (March 2005). *Race, culture, power, and inclusion in foundations*. Retrieved from: www.philanthropy.iupui.edu/Millennium/usefulInformation/Race%20%20Culture%20%20Power%20%20Inclusionin%20Foundations.pdf.

Marquez, B. (1993). *LULAC: The evolution of a Mexican American political organization*. Austin, TX: University of Texas Press.

Marx, J. & Carter, V. B. (2008). Hispanic charitable giving: An opportunity for nonprofit development. *Nonprofit Management & Leadership*, 19(2), 173–87.

Messenbourg, T. (June 8, 2011). A new benchmark for minority business ownership. Retrieved from: http://blogs.census.gov/2011/06/08/a-new-benchmark-for-minority-business-ownership/.

Miranda, J. (1999). Religion, philanthropy, and the Hispanic people in North America. *New Directions for Philanthropic Fundraising*, 24, 59–73.

Moss, L. B., Genia, T., & Jennings, M. (April 4, 2011). *Improving foundation grantmaking outcomes in Indian country* [PowerPoint slides]. Retrieved from Northwest Area Foundation website: www.nativephilanthropy.org/system/files/user/NWAF%20Presentation%20for%20Native%20Vision%20at%202011%20NPI.pdf.

Mottino, F. & Miller, E. D. (September 2004). *Pathway for change: Philanthropy among African American, Asian American, and Latino donors in the New York metropolitan region*. Retrieved from the Center on Philanthropy and Civil Society website: www.philanthropy.org/programs/documents/PathwaysforChange_ExecSummary_000.pdf.

Mukai, R., Lawrence, S., Delgado, L. T., & Hicks, S. (2011). *Foundation funding for Native American issues and peoples*. Retrieved from The Foundation Center website: www.nativephilanthropy.org/system/files/user/2011%20Foundation%20Funding%20for%20Native%20American%20Issues%20and%20Peoples_0.pdf.

Multilateral Investment Fund Inter-American Development Bank (2003). *Sending money home: An international comparison of remittance markets*. New York: Multilateral Investment Fund Inter-American Development Bank.

Nash, G. B. (1991). *Forging freedom: The formation of Philadelphia's black community, 1720–1840*. Cambridge, MA: Harvard University Press.

National Center for Education Statistics (2010). www.nces.gov.

National Center for Education Statistics (2012). www.nces.gov.

Native Americans in Philanthropy (2004). *2004 annual report*. Retrieved from Native Americans in Philanthropy website: www.nativephilanthropy.org/sites/nativephilanthropy.org/files/user/2004_Annual_Report.pdf.

Native Americans in Philanthropy (2006). *2006 annual report*. Retrieved from Native Americans in Philanthropy website: www.nativephilanthropy.org/sites/nativephilanthropy.org/files/user/NAP_annual_report_06.pdf.

Native Americans in Philanthropy (2008). *2007–2008 annual report*. Retrieved from

Native Americans in Philanthropy website: http://nativephilanthropy.org/sites/nativephilanthropy.org/files/user/NAP_Annual_Report_2008_0.pdf.

Native Americans in Philanthropy (2011). *Weaving leadership, indigenous people & resources: 2011 Annual member meeting* [PowerPoint slide]. Retrieved from: www.nativephilanthropy.org/system/files/user/2011%20Annual%20Meeting_0.pdf.

Naya, S. (2007) Income distribution and poverty alleviation for the Native Hawaiian community. Paper presented at the 2nd Annual Hawaiian Business Conference, Honolulu, May 2007. *A new heritage of giving philanthropy in Asian America* (2012). Retrieved from: http://asian americanphilanthropy.org/default.asp.

Newman, D. S. (1999). The role of community foundation in establishing and growing endowment funds by and for diverse ethnic communities. Retrieved from: www.cof.org/files/Documents/Publications/Cultures_of_Caring/roleofcommfdns.pdf.

Newman, D. S., Berry, M., Chao, J., Ramos, H. A. J., &. Winters, M. F. (2002). *Opening doors: Pathways to diverse donors*. San Francisco, CA: Jossey-Bass.

Nichols, J. E. (1997). Fundraising in the USA and the United Kingdom: Comparing today with directions for tomorrow. *International Journal of Nonprofit and Voluntary Sector Marketing*, 2(2), 148–53. doi: 10.1002/nvsm.6090020206.

Nichols, J. E. (2004). Repositioning fundraising in the 21st century. *International Journal of Nonprofit and Voluntary Sector Marketing*, 9(2), 163–70. doi: 10.1002/nvsm.244.

Nichols, J. (2008). *Diversity and donors: Understanding your minority prospects*. Causeplanet.org, www.causeplanet.org.

Nielsen Report (2011). *The state of the African American consumer*. New York: Nielsen.

Nielsen, J., Hovila, N., & Nielsen, J. (2010). *Changing the Native philanthropic landscape: A study on mainstream philanthropic board participation.* Nielsen and Associates Applied Research and Evaluation.

Norton, L. P. (December 9, 2002). Asian-American giving—the Chinese connection: A new force is emerging in the philanthropic world. *Dow Jones & Company Inc.* Retrieved from: www.committee100.org/media/media_eng/120902.html.

O'Conor, W. J. (2007). *Factors that motivate Hispanics donors to philanthropically support higher education* (Doctoral Dissertation, State University of New York at Buffalo). Retrieved from Dissertation and Theses database. (ProQuest No. 3262004).

Okten, C. & Osili, U. O. (n.d.). *Ethnic diversity and charitable giving.* Retrieved from: www.phildev.iupui.edu/Millennium/usefulInformation/Ethnic%20Diversity%20and%20Charitable%20Giving.pdf.

Olsen, L. (1997). *An invisible crisis: The education needs of Asian Pacific American youth.* San Francisco, CA: Asian American/Pacific Islander in Philanthropy. Retrieved from ERIC database. (ED416273).

Onishi, T. (2007). Japanese fundraising: A comparative study of the United States and Japan. *International Journal of Educational Advancement*, 7, 205–25.

Osili, U. O. & Du, D. (2005). Immigrant assimilation and charitable giving. *New Directions for Philanthropic Fundraising*, 48, 89–104. Retrieved from: www.philanthropy.iupui.edu/lakefamilyinstitute/UnaOsili.pdf.

Parra, O. V. (1999). Hispanic women: Nurturing tomorrow's philanthropy. *New Directions for Philanthropic Fundraising*, 24, 75–84. doi: 10.1002/pf.2405.

Patton, L. (2010). *Cultural centers in higher education: Perspectives on identity, theory, and practice.* Sterling, VA: Stylus Press.

Pease, K. (2003). *Inside inclusiveness: Race, ethnicity and nonprofit organizations.* Retrieved from the Denver Foundation website: www.philanthropy.iupui.edu/Millennium/usefulInformation/Inside%20Inclusiveness%20Race%20Ethnicity%20and%20Nonprofit%20Organization.pdf.

Pettey, J. G. (2001). *Cultivating diversity in fund-raising.* San Francisco, CA: Jossey-Bass.

Pettey, J. G. (2002). Can remittances increase charitable giving among immigrant families? *New Directions for Philanthropic Fundraising*, 37, 35–44.

Pettey, J. G. & Wagner, L. (2007). Introduction: Union gives strength—diversity and fundraising. *International Journal of Education Advancement*, 7, 171–5. doi: 10.1057/palgrave.ijea2150059.

Pew Hispanic Center (2010). *Statistical portrait of Hispanics in the United States*. Washington, DC: Research Center.

Pew Research Center (2012). *The rise of Asian Americans*. Washington, DC: Pew Research Center.

Pittz, W. & Sen, R. (n.d.). *Short changed: Foundation giving and communities of color*. Retrieved from Applied Research Center website: www.arc.org/pdf/273bpdf.pdf.

Pressley, C. O. (1995). Financial contributions for the kingdom from the elect: Giving patterns in the black church. *New Directions for Philanthropic Fundraising*, 7, 91–100. doi: 10.1002/pf.41219950708.

Ramos, H. A. J. (1999). *Latino philanthropy: Expanding U.S. models of giving and civic participation*. Berkeley, CA: Mauer Kunst Consulting.

Ramos, H. & Kasper, G. (2000). *Building a tradition of Latino philanthropy: Hispanics as donors, grantees, grantmakers, and volunteers*. Center for Philanthropy and Public Policy.

Ridings, D. S. (1997). Philanthropy in action: Building community. *National Civic Review*, 86(4), 281–6. doi: 10.1002/ncr.4100860404.

Rodriguez, C. (1999). Education and Hispanic philanthropy: Family, sacrifice, and community. *New Directors for Philanthropic Fundraising*, 24, 41–57.

Rooney, P.J. & Sherman, L. (eds.). (2005). Exploring black philanthropy. *New Directions for Philanthropic Fundraising*, 48, 1–122. doi: 10.1002/pf.v2005.48.

Rothwell, D. W. (2011). The case for asset based interventions with indigenous peoples: Evidence from Hawaii. *International Social Work*, 54(1), 35–50.

Royce, A. & Rodriguez, R. (1999). From personal charity to organized giving: Hispanic institutions and values of stewardship and philanthropy. *New Directions for Philanthropic Fundraising*, 24, 9–29.

Sanchez, D. & Zamora, R. (1999). Current issues affecting U.S. Hispanic foundations and nonprofit directors/trustees: A survey of the field. In D. Campoamor, W. A. Diaz, & H. A. J. Ramos (eds.), *Nuevos Senderos: Reflections on Hispanic and philanthropy*, pp. 77–93. Houston, TX: Arte Publico.

Schneewind, J. B. (ed.). (1996). *Giving: Western ideas of philanthropy*. Bloomington, IN: Indiana University Press.

Schneider, S. W. & von Schlegell, G. (1993). Richness in diversity. *New Directions for Philanthropic Fundraising*, 2, 135–41. doi: 10.1002/pf.41219 932012.

Selig Center for Economic Growth (2009). *The multi-cultural economy*. Athens, GA: University of Georgia.

Shao, S. (1995). Asian American giving: Issues and challenges (a practitioner's perspective). *New Directions for Philanthropic Fundraising*, 8, 53–64. doi: 10.1002/pf41219950806.

Shiao, J. L. (2004). *Identifying talent, institutionalizing diversity: Race and philanthropy in post-civil rights America*. Durham, NC: Duke University Press.

Siciliano, J. (1996). The relationship of board member diversity to organizational performance. *Journal of Business Ethics*, 15(12), 1313–20.

Singer, M., Flores, C., Davison, L., Burke, G., & Castillo, Z. (1991). Puerto Rican community mobilizing in response to the AIDS crisis. *Human Organization*, 50(1), 74–81. Retrieved from: http://sfaa.metapress.com/link.asp?id=t2p0t06604530475.

Smith, B., Shue, S., Vest, J., & Villarreal, J. (1999). *Philanthropy in communities of color*. Bloomington, IN: Indiana University Press.

Steinberg, R. & Wilhelm, M. (2005). Religious and secular giving by race and ethnicity. *New Directions for Philanthropic Fundraising*, 48, 57–66.

Swierzewski, R. (August 2007). *Rural philanthropy: Building dialogue from within*. Retrieved from National Committee for Responsive Philanthropy website: www.philanthropy.iupui.edu/Millennium/usefulInformation/Rural%20Philanthropy%20-%20Dialogue%20Within.pdf.

Terrell, M. C., Rudy, D. E., & Cheatham, H. E. (1993). The role of external funding for cultural diversity programming. *New Directions for Student Services*, 63, 75–84. doi: 10.1002/ss.37119936309.

Tindal, N. T. J. (2009). Working on the short grass: A qualitative analysis of fundraiser roles and experiences at public historically black colleges and universities. *International Journal of Educational Advancement*, 9, 3–15. doi: 10.1057/ijea.2009.17.

Tokumura, S. (2001). Fundraising mores in diverse communities: The role of ethnicity and culture. *New Directions for Philanthropic Fundraising*, 34, 3–30.

Tsunoda, K. (2010). Asian American giving to U.S. higher education. *International Journal of Educational Advancement*, 10(1), 2–23.

U.S. Census (2010). Retrieved from: www.census.gov.

Wagner, L. & Hall-Russell, C. (1999). The effectiveness of fundraising training in Hispanic religious organizations. *New Directions for Philanthropic Fundraising*, 24, 85–105.

Wagner, L. & Ryan, J. P. (2004). Achieving diversity among fundraising professionals. *New Directions for Philanthropic Fundraising*, 41, 63–70.

Wallenstein, P. (2008). *Higher education and the Civil Rights Movement: White supremacy, Black southerners, and college campuses*. Gainesville, FL: University Press of Florida.

Wilkinson-Maposa, S., Fowler, A., Oliver-Evans, C., and Mulenga, C. F. N. (n.d.). *The poor philanthropist: How and why the poor help each other*. Retrieved from: www.philanthropy.iupui.edu/Millennium/useful Information/The%20Poor%20Philanthropist%20(South%20Africa).pdf.

Williams, H. (2005). *Self-taught: African American education in slavery and freedom*. Chapel Hill, NC: University of North Carolina Press.

Willie, C. V. (1981). Philanthropic and foundation support for blacks: A case study from the 1960s. *The Journal of Negro Education*, 50(3), 270–84. Retrieved from: www.jstor.org/stable/2295157.

Winters, M. F. (1999). Reflections on endowment building in the African American community. In *Cultures of caring: Philanthropy in diverse American communities*, pp. 77–93. Washington, DC: Council on Foundations.

W. K. Kellogg Foundation (2001). *Emerging philanthropy in communities of color: A report on emerging trends*. Michigan: Kellogg Foundation.

W. K. Kellogg Foundation (2012). *Cultures of giving: Energizing and expanding philanthropy by and for communities of color*. Michigan: Kellogg Foundation.

Woods, A. (2011) in Hunt, E. (n.d.). African American philanthropy: A legacy of giving. Retrieved from the Twenty-First Century Foundation website: www.21cf.org/pdf/LegacyOfGiving.

Yin, X. (2004). A case study of transnationalism continuity and changes in Chinese American philanthropy to China. *American Studies*, 45(2), 65–99.

INDEX